CW01335909

Wanstead

and its

Park

by

Oliver S. Dawson

with additional material

by

Richard Arnopp

Published by the Friends of Wanstead Parklands
www.wansteadpark.org.uk
© Copyright: Friends of Wanstead Parklands 2014
ISBN: 978-1-291-66098-2

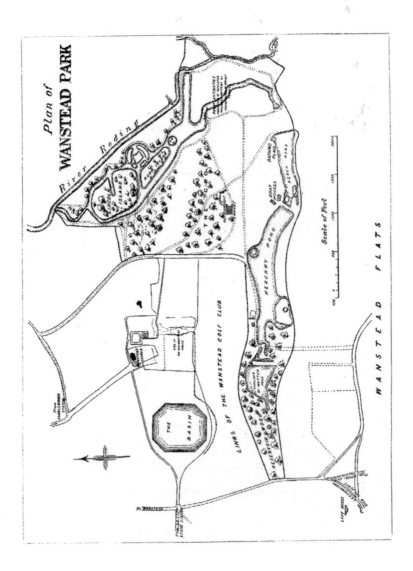

Plan of
WANSTEAD PARK

CONTENTS

Introduction i

Oliver S. Dawson: a biographical note iii

Notes on the text x

Wanstead and its Park 1

Endnotes 66

LIST OF MAPS, PHOTOGRAPHS AND PRINTS

Map: Wanstead Park — Inside front cover

Photograph: *Near Lincoln Island - in autumn* — 1

Print: *King Edward VI, from an old engraving* — 4

Print: *Queen Mary, from an old painting* — 5

Print: *Queen Elizabeth, from an old engraving* — 6

Print: *Robert, Earl of Leicester, from an old engraving* — 7

Print: *View of Wanstead House* — 34

Photograph: *The Bathing Lake, Wanstead Park* — 37

Photograph: *The Grotto from the lake side - in autumn* — 39

Photograph: *Interior of Grotto before the fire* — 42

Photograph: *The Water Gate - Grotto* — 44

Photograph: *The home of the herons* — 47

Photograph: *Evelyn Avenue, Bush Wood* — 50

Photograph: *Perch Pond - in early spring* — 53

Photograph: *The refreshment chalet* — 57

INTRODUCTION

Wanstead and its Park was published in instalments in *The Home Counties Magazine* during 1907 and 1908. The text was adapted and expanded from a booklet entitled *The Story of Wanstead Park* which the author, Oliver S. Dawson, had first published in 1894.

The Wanstead estate, over several centuries, was associated with a remarkable cast of characters, including the Tudor monarchs, the unfortunate Sir Giles Heron, the great Earl of Leicester, the regicide Sir Henry Mildmay and the formidable Sir Josiah Child and his family. Though Oliver Dawson did not aspire to produce a work of original scholarship, he nonetheless performed a useful service in putting together an accessible introduction to the story of the park's owners and its early days as a public open space.

Oliver Dawson was not a native of Wanstead, and settled there only when he was aged around 40, around the time that *The Story of Wanstead Park* appeared in print. However, he was no stranger to the area. Originally from Buckinghamshire, he had moved to West Ham in the 1870s. Apart from a brief sojourn in Mortlake in the early 1890s, Dawson spent the rest of his life in suburban Essex.

The purchase of Wanstead Park by the Corporation of the City of London in 1882, and its opening to the public, may well have been what prompted Dawson's first stirrings of curiosity about its history. In the 1880s, the downfall of the last resident owners, the demolition of their "princely mansion" and the despoliation of the estate were still within living memory, and Dawson may even have met first-hand witnesses to these events.

Be that as it may, Oliver Dawson himself was certainly a witness to the public park in its very earliest days, and the charming photographs which illustrated his 1894 booklet give us a good impression of what it was like when he knew it.

The Friends of Wanstead Parklands are dedicated to raising awareness of Wanstead Park and its heritage, and we hope that our re-publication of this interesting period piece, with some new material to remedy its defects and increase its usefulness, will help to further this end. This edition includes some new material about Oliver Dawson's own life, as well as a comprehensive set of endnotes to assist the modern reader.

Richard Arnopp
Friends of Wanstead Parklands
2014

OLIVER S. DAWSON: A BIOGRAPHICAL NOTE

Oliver Dawson had a fascinating life, which might have been taken from the pages of Samuel Smiles' Victorian classic *Self-Help*. Having started out as a manual worker, he educated himself, went into business and eventually became something of a pioneer of colour photography.

Dawson was born in 1854 in Wolverton, Buckinghamshire, a small town which has since been swallowed by the growth of Milton Keynes. On the evidence of the 1851 and 1861 censuses, it appears that the family must have settled in Wolverton at some time between 1848 and 1851, having moved from Stony Stratford, a short distance away.

Most residents of Young Street, where the family were living at this time, seem to have had occupations connected to the railway. According to the Milton Keynes Heritage Association -

When Robert Stephenson (1803 - 59) brought the London & Birmingham Railway through in 1838, (part of the London & North Western Railway from1846) the Wolverton area was largely green fields, although the canal had already been constructed. 'Wolverton', later to be called 'Old Wolverton', was a community of around 400 over towards Stony Stratford. When the railway came, the area built around it was known as 'Wolverton Station' but rapidly developed into the 'new' Wolverton.

Stephenson chose Wolverton to provide a site roughly half way between London Euston and Birmingham Curzon Street for the servicing and refuelling of locomotives. The line also conveniently bisected the Grand Junction Canal here too and supplies to build the new railway town were transported by barge. As the population grew to carry out these tasks, so did the town, with many of the new streets (e. g. Bury Street, Young Street, Creed Street, Glyn Square) being named after railway officials.

Oliver Dawson's father, Samuel, was himself a railway porter. In the 1861 Census, Samuel's age was given as 38, and his place of birth as Banbury in

Oxfordshire. His wife Mary was older - 44 - and originally from Whatfield in Northamptonshire. Oliver, then aged 7, was the youngest of the four children then living at home. The others were Thomas, aged 18, a boiler maker; Temperance, aged 16; and Edwin, aged 11. There was also a boarder, James Austley, aged 16, an engine stoker. A further child, George, who had appeared in the 1851 census aged 3, was not listed in 1861 or thereafter, having presumably died in the interim.

By 1871, Samuel and Mary had moved to another property, in Sharp Road. There were also two lodgers living with them. Of their children only Oliver (now aged 17) was still at home. By now, Samuel was described as foreman of a goods yard, and Oliver as an apprentice fitter. Oliver's two brothers and sister had left the area, presumably for reasons connected with work or marriage. However, Samuel was to remain in Wolverton until his death in 1893. His biblical given name, and the choice of "Temperance" for his daughter, may hint that the family were Nonconformists, though there is currently no other evidence for this.

At some time in the 1870s, Oliver Dawson moved to London. The 1881 Census shows an important change in his circumstances. He was now 27 years old and, like his three siblings, had left Wolverton and married. Where Dawson's situation differed from the rest of his family was that he had left manual labour behind, and was working as a solicitor's clerk. In an article he published in 1891[1], Dawson provides a clue as to how he had achieved this. In making a plea for adult education not to become too centralised in large institutions, he refers to the Science and Art Institute, Wolverton, as "one of the best and most practical schools in the country". At the end of the article he says, surely with personal feeling "To the working man with limited time and means, weary with his day's toil, a modest school close at hand is of greater service than a huge building six miles away involving railway fare and loss of time". Local press reports between 1869 and 1875 confirm Dawson's attendance at the Science and

---

[1] *Nature* 8 December 1891 *The Existing Schools of Science and Art* by Oliver S Dawson

Art Institute, and allow one to track the progress of his studies in mathematics and a number of technical subjects.

The Wolverton Institute began as a Mechanics Institute in 1840, and is worthy of note as having been only the second institution of this kind in the country[2]. For many years it was without any permanent buildings: the Reading Room beside the canal served as a place for lectures and a library, and it was not until 1864 that a dedicated building was available. Re-named at this time the Wolverton Science and Art Institute, it had 12 classrooms, a library, an auditorium and a lecture theatre. Evening classes were offered in a range of disciplines. The building was sadly destroyed by fire in 1970.

In 1881 Oliver Dawson was living in West Ham with his wife, Florence, then aged 22, and their first child. They had married in 1878, in Islington.

Florence Ellen Holden was one of at least six children born to Henry Holden, a tailor, and his wife Ellen. Henry Holden originally came from Horsley in Derbyshire, where some of his children had been born. In 1871 the family was living at 263 Grays Inn Road. Henry was evidently successful in business, as in 1871 he was employing 6 men and a woman. Henry Holden was probably the individual of that name whose death in 1875 was registered in the Pancras district. The death of one Ellen Holden was registered in 1878 in the same district. It may be that the death of both of her parents was one of the factors that prompted Florence's early marriage to Dawson - she would have been about 19 at the time. Otherwise this would have been somewhat unusual, especially given the difference in the circumstances of their respective families.

Park Grove, where the Dawsons had their home at this time, is a turning off Portway, south of West Ham Park. It was very close to Stratford Road, where Dawson's sister Temperance and her family were then living, and the Dawsons no doubt chose it for that reason. In recent decades Park Grove has been swallowed up in a large council estate. However, in the 1880s it

---

[2] The first was Owen's College, which later became the University of Manchester.

was part of a newly-built residential area of modestly comfortable terraced and semi-detached houses, many of which still survive in nearby streets.

Three children were born to the Dawsons' marriage, all in West Ham. Oliver Trevelyan Dawson was born in the third quarter of 1879. Harold Evelyn Dawson was born in the fourth quarter of 1883. Hilda Fanny was born in the second quarter of 1889.

By 1891, the family had temporarily left the eastern suburbs of London and had settled at 2 Alder Villas, Mortlake. This was presumably the present-day Alder Road, not far from Mortlake Station. Oliver Dawson's occupation had again changed and was now given as "engraver". The family were now sufficiently well-off to employ a live-in servant, Eliza Collins, aged 17.

Prior to the 1890s, our impressions of Oliver Dawson are mostly derived from the limited and stereotyped records of the census. However, from that time we start to see occasional glimpses of a more rounded, flesh and blood figure. We have already referred to an article he published in 1891. On 7 March 1892 Dawson appeared as a witness in a case at the Old Bailey. This was his evidence -

OLIVER SAMUEL DAWSON. "I am an engineer and zincographer at 35, Essex Street, Strand - my firm engraved all the blocks that illustrated the *British Building Journal*, the prisoner's paper - he first employed us about the beginning of April, 1891; there were twelve issues of the paper altogether, I think - I know nothing of its financial position - we have not been paid a farthing for what we did - my firm are creditors for something over £30 in the bankruptcy proceedings that have been taken against the prisoner - we gave the prisoner a certain amount of credit, and when we pressed for payment he called and produced a telegram which purported to be an offer of some thousands for certain property at Greenhithe, which he explained he was selling, and that we should soon be paid - I formed the opinion from what he said that he had received an offer for certain property of his own - I cannot say whether he said it was his own-he gave us a bill which was dishonoured".

It was in the 1890s that Dawson and his family moved to Wanstead, perhaps another indication of their increasing prosperity. The introduction to a previous edition of *The Story of Wanstead Park* stated "We do know that he did not live in Wanstead until 1894 when he moved into "Bardons" 18 Mansfield Road, which was then a newly built private house on the Oak Hall Estate". We can only speculate about what prompted Dawson to produce his booklet about Wanstead Park at this time. It may, of course, have been simply the product of personal enthusiasm. However, Dawson was a man of entrepreneurial spirit, and it may also have been a business venture, to cater to the large number of visitors to the park.

In the 1901 census Oliver Dawson was still resident at 18 Mansfield Road, along with his wife and three children. He and his sons were all described as photo-engravers on zinc and copper. He was designated as an "employer" and his sons as "workers".

By the time of the 1911 census the family were renting a larger property, known as Fir Tree Cottage in George Lane. George Lane is now known as Nutter Lane, re-named after the family of local benefactors who formerly lived at Applegarth House. Fir Tree Cottage - of which photographs still exist - was demolished during the early 1930s, and has since been replaced by numbers 12-18. Oliver Dawson and his sons - who were both at this time still single - were this time described on the Census return as "photographic materials makers". Dawson was designated as an "employer" and his sons as "workmen". His daughter Hilda, by now aged 22 and also single, was described as a teacher employed by the Borough Council. The household included a general domestic servant, Agnes Page.

The following is from *The British Journal Of Photography*, from 1911, and relates to Oliver Samuel Dawson and his son "Treves" -

CROYDON CAMERA CLUB. "As an example of a straightforward and thoroughly practical demonstration, the exposition of Mr. Treves Dawson last week on the Thames colour-plate could hardly have been bettered. Among the large and appreciative audience was Mr. O. S. Dawson, who, quietly smoking a pipe in a corner, listened with the closest attention, and with evident gratification, to all his son had to say.

The strong points of the plate in question and the general procedure for obtaining colour records being well known, need not be alluded to, but one or two points arose deserving of mention. Many excellent slides were shown, but under the electric-arc projection it was noticed that the greens of foliage and grass were generally rendered distinctly on the blue side, rather opposed to Nature's tints and inimical to a feeling of sunshine. Some rough experiments tried by placing yellow filters in front of the projection lens seemed to indicate that a compensating filter of a very light yellow hue would be of advantage in toning down the greens, especially in those cases where there were no pure blues which might suffer degradation in con- sequence. The screens at hand were of far too deep a tint for any definite conclusion to be arrived at, but even they undoubtedly improved one or two slides in which the greens and reds pre- dominated ; conversely in others where blues were prominent".

"Mr. Dawson strongly recommended the "separate method " on various grounds, and certainly everything seemed in favour of this system, except that the subsequent registration and binding-up of the two plates appeared to require considerable dexterity. The lecturer, however, said this difficulty was more apparent than real, and registered two in the lantern, eliciting applause as a pretty little girl suddenly emerged from a medley of colours in a bright blue dress. "That is quite incorrect," Mr. Dawson observed quietly, "the dress was red," and, with a further minute shift, red it was. It was recommended that one or two screens should be solely applied to "taking" purposes, and one for temporary registration to judge results by visual inspection. Sometimes only a small portion of a large plate might be required; in such a case a small-size screen-plate obviously was only requisite, thereby limiting expense. In answer to a question it was stated that the cost of a finished lantern plate, all being well, was 10d. Mr. Keane said he had been employing the Thames colour-plate in night photography in conjunction with a K 1 filter, which for this class of work seemed all that was necessary. The exposures required were by no means as long as might be anticipated; with a large aperture and on suitable subjects, exposures of one to five minutes gave excellent results".

The *British Journal Of Photography* refers also to patents obtained by Oliver S. Dawson and Clare Livingstone Finlay relating to the process of making colour screens. It appears that Finlay was his collaborator for some years.

Half way through the First World War, on 27 May 1916, Oliver Dawson died at Fir Tree Cottage, after suffering from heart problems. He was 62 years old, and his last occupation was given on his death certificate as "photographer". Dawson's widow Florence was granted administration of his effects, to the value of £342. In the 2 June edition of the *British Journal of Photography* there appeared an obituary which stated that, although his business ventures in the field of colour photography had been hampered by production problems, he had latterly "occupied himself with experimental work in cinematography".

Oliver Dawson's death at least meant he was spared the calamity which befell his family the following year. In December 1917, his elder son "Treves", by now married and living in Ilford, was killed in action in northern France, aged 38, at the Battle of Cambrai. Like so many others, he has no known grave, and is remembered with more than 7,000 servicemen of the United Kingdom and South Africa on the Cambrai Memorial, Louverval. Dawson's other son, Harold, continued the family involvement in photography, and lived in Leybourne Road, Leytonstone, until his death in 1970. The last of Oliver Dawson's children, his daughter Hilda, died unmarried in 1974.

NOTES ON THE TEXT

This publication is a hybrid, comprising elements of both versions of Oliver Dawson's work.

The text is taken from the later and slightly more detailed of the two, which appeared in *The Home Counties Magazine* Volume IX (1907) pp45-51, 168-172, 276-280; and Volume X (1908) pp64-69, 77, 137-143, 227-233, 275-285. The few footnotes included by Oliver S. Dawson or his editor have been reproduced as they appeared, but numbered as a single series rather than by page.

The illustrations are taken from Dawson's 1894 booklet *The Story of Wanstead Park*, though they have been moved around in relation to the text. The original advertisements from the booklet are also included at the end as a group, for their interest and period quality.

A large number of endnotes have been added for the convenience of the modern reader, and are indicated in the text by Roman numerals. They are intended to be free-standing, and may be browsed without reference to the main text. Their primary purpose is to provide additional information on matters covered by Dawson, as well as correcting a few errors which crept into his text. However, the opportunity has been taken to include additional notes on most of the prominent individuals who are mentioned in Dawson's pages, to provide some historical context. Also included are notes on aspects of the park and its development, about which Dawson says relatively little. Some local references are explained, along with archaic terms which are no longer generally understood. A few points are included for no other reason than that they appeared curious or interesting to the present editor.

NEAR LINCOLN ISLAND—IN AUTUMN.

WANSTEAD AND ITS PARK
BY OLIVER S. DAWSON

THE village of Wanstead is situated on the borders of Waltham Forest[i]. It stands upon a hill which once commanded a view of the City of London and its environs; the hills of Kent, the river Thames, and a wide expanse of highly cultivated and beautiful scenery can still be seen. The village consisted of a long straggling street, lying between Snaresbrook[ii] Station and the Park, but although a few picturesque old houses still remain, the district is rapidly assuming the usual characteristics of a suburb of London.

At the end of the village nearest to the Park stands the George Inn[iii]. In the wall of this hostelry is a stone, bearing the date. 1752, to commemorate a somewhat ludicrous event which happened there. The inscription, which was restored in 1858, runs as follows:-

1

*"In memorie of ye cherry pie
As cost ½ a guinea 17th of July;
That day we had good cheer,
And hope so to do many a year.
R. D. 1752. Dad. Terry."*

The story is that some workmen were engaged in doing some alterations at the house on the above date, and while they were at work a pie was sent from the Rectory to the baking shop next door to the George, as is still the custom in country districts. As the pie was being borne home, one of the workmen leaned over from the scaffold, and took it off the baker's tray, and doubtless they enjoyed the feast all the more since it was stolen. For this little joke they were brought before the local magistrate, and fined half-a-guinea, which was duly paid.

On leaving the court, the men decided to place this stone in the wall to commemorate the event, each contributing a small sum to pay for it.

Before the days of Local Boards[iv], it was only by the liberality of private individuals that obvious public benefits could be provided. It is interesting to note, therefore, that the stone bridge at Wanstead, over the Roding, is still kept in order by the income from land bequeathed for that purpose hundreds of years ago.

How the name of Wanstead originated is not clearly known[v]. According to one authority, it is derived from the Saxon words Wan and Stead, signifying a white place or mansion. A more recent opinion, however, supposes it to be a corruption of Woden-stead, a name implying the existence here of a mound or other erection dedicated to the worship of Woden[3].

The earliest known record of Waenstede is the grant of it by one Alfric to St. Peter's Church (afterward Westminster Abbey), which gift was confirmed by Edward the Confessor[vi] in 1066. At some date between the Conquest and 1087, it became, probably by exchange, the property of the Church of St.

---

[3] It is more likely derived from the personal name of an early owner. Wana, Wanes, Wenning, and other similar personal names, are to be found in Domesday. Wain is still a common English surname.—EDITOR.

Paul (now St. Paul's Cathedral), and was afterwards appropriated to the Bishop of London, under whom, at the time of the Domes-day Survey, it was held by Ralph Fitz-Brien[vii]. The following is a translation from Domesday[viii] Book:-

LAND OF THE BISHOP OF LONDON.

HUNDRED OF BEUENTREV [Becontree][ix].

St. Paul held Wanesteda, now Ralph son of Brien [holds it] of the Bishop for one manor[x] and one hide. Then [i. e. in the time of Edward the Confessor] one plough in demesne ; now one and a half. Always [i. e. then and now] two ploughs of the men, and three villeins. Then seven bordars[xi]; now eight. Then two serfs[xii]; now none. Wood for 300 pigs. Now one mill. Always one salt-pan.
And it is worth 40s.-(Domesday Book, vol. 2, fo. 9 b.)

The manor had improved since Saxon days. The lord ploughed more land, half as much again; the bordars, cottagers or crofters, had increased from seven to eight; the two serfs had disappeared; and a mill had been built. We are not told the former yearly value, but it was probably less than its Domesday value of 40s.

It will be noticed that salt-works[xiii] are mentioned, and old maps show that salt-making by evaporation of sea water was practised on the Essex coast in very early times. The works at Wanstead were probably for refining purposes.[4]

---

[4] See H. C. M., vol. viii, p. 269, for a note on the early Essex salt-pans.— EDITOR.

From Ralph Fitz-Brien the estate passed to the de Hoding[xiv] family, and by marriage to William de Huntercombe[xv], who died in 1271 ; his descendants held it from the time of Henry III until towards the close of the reign of Richard II. In 1446 John Tattershall[xvi] held it, and he was succeeded by Robert Tattershall and others, and in 1487 by Sir Ralph Hastings[xvii]; the manor afterwards passed to Sir John Heron. His son, Sir Giles Heron[xviii], who married the daughter of the worthy but hapless Sir Thomas More[xix], was, in the reign of Henry VIII[xx], attainted of treason, because he would not acknowledge the King's supremacy as the head of the

KING EDWARD VI., FROM AN OLD ENGRAVING.

Church[xxi]. His estates were seized by the Crown, and this manor was granted in 1549 by Edward VI to Richard, Lord Rich[xxii], who made it his country seat, and is supposed to have rebuilt the manor house, then called Naked Hall Hawe.

It is evident that at this period the house at Wanstead was one of the most important in this part of the country, for we find it closely identified with English history.

On August 1st, 1553, Queen Mary[xxiii] arrived at Wanstead in her progress from Norwich to London to assume the crown. Her brother, King Edward VI[xxiv], had died on the 6th of July, 1553, and the Duke of Northumberland[xxv], the head of the reformed religion (Protestant), had persuaded the young King just before his death (he was only sixteen when

4

he died) to sign a paper appointing Lady Jane Grey[xxvi] to be his successor to the throne, thus setting aside the rights of both the Princesses Mary and Elizabeth.

The friends of Mary had informed her of this, and she accordingly escaped to Norwich.

Lady Jane Grey's dream of royalty lasted exactly ten days. She had not sought it, and she gladly resigned it. Mary started from Norwich for London, and it was at Wanstead House that she broke her journey to receive her sister, the Princess Elizabeth, who rode out of London attended by a train of a thousand knights,

QUEEN ELIZABETH, FROM AN OLD ENGRAVING.

ladies, and gentlemen, to meet the Queen. It must have been a strange meeting. Mary was a Catholic, Elizabeth was a Protestant. The home that sheltered them had been taken, as mentioned above, by their father, Henry VIII, from its owner, Sir Giles Heron, because of his adherence to the Catholic faith, and this monarch had also beheaded Sir Thomas More, the father of Heron's wife, who personally accompanied her father to the scaffold, and was present at his execution. I wonder if Mary and Elizabeth slept well at the mansion! I fancy that if my father had so served its late owner and his relative, I should have passed a very bad night.

From Wanstead the two Princesses passed on August 3rd to the Tower of London, and there the Queen first kissed and then liberated the prisoners

5

ROBBERT DUDLEY.
GRAAF VAN LEICESTER.

ROBERT, EARL OF LEICESTER, FROM AN OLD ENGRAVING.

who were confined because they were Catholics; and in course of time she filled the dungeons with the adherents of the reformed faith.

Mary was thirty-seven years of age when she ascended the throne, and she reigned for not quite five-and-a-half years, dying in 1558. Elizabeth succeeded her at the age of twenty- five, and with this Queen the history of Wanstead is again connected with the royal house, for she visited Lord Rich there on July 14th, 1561. Robert, 2nd Lord Rich[xxvii], son of the former grantee, sold Wanstead, in 1577, to the notorious Robert Dudley, Earl of Leicester[xxviii], Knight of the Garter, and afterwards Governor of the Netherlands, who enlarged and greatly improved the mansion.

This nobleman was a great favourite of the Queen; indeed, there seems good ground for believing that she would at one time have married him if he had not already had a wife. When the *Invincible Armada* was expected, and Elizabeth reviewed and addressed the troops at Tilbury Fort[xxix], it was Leicester who held her bridle rein.

In May, 1578, Queen Elizabeth paid a visit of five days to Leicester at Wanstead House, and great things were done by way of entertainment for her. Sir Philip Sidney[xxx], the eldest son of Leicester's sister, Mary, wrote a

6

masque in honour of the occasion, entitled "The Queen of May," in which the virtue and beauty of the Queen was lauded to the skies. The dialogue of this curious performance is printed in Nichols' *Progresses of Queen Elizabeth*.

A picture of the Queen is still to be seen at Welbeck Abbey, the country seat of the Duke of Portland, which contains as a background a view of Wanstead House as it appeared on this occasion.

Leicester's first wife, the hapless Amy Robsart[xxxi], died on September 8th, 1560. His second wife was Lettice[xxxii], daughter of Sir Francis Knolles, and widow of Walter Devereux, Earl of Essex[xxxiii]; the marriage was a private one, and took place at Wanstead House on September 21st, 1578. The following account of the ceremony was given by Ambrose Dudley, Earl of Warwick[xxxiv], Leicester's brother, in 1581.

> *"That he [Warwick], beinge Brother to the Erle of Leicester and very familier wth him and his affaires, was by him made acquainted wth the good love and likeinge grounded betweene him and the Countesse of Essex, and lastlie how he was resolved to make her his wief. Wheruppon this Deponent for the dispatch therof, at the request of his said Brother, uppon a Satterdaie (as he now remembreth) came to Wainsted House (her Ma[ty] then lyinge, as far as he likewise remembreth, at one Stoner's in Waltham Forrest), in w[ch] house (as he sayth) and in a litle Gallery therof, the next morninge followinge (beinge, as he nowe remembreth, the xxjth daie of September in Anno D[ni] 1578) his said brother and the said Countesse of Essex were marryed together, after the order of the Booke of Comon Prayers, by one Mr. Tindall, a servaunt and chaplein to his brother Leicester, in such like manner and forme as other folkes are accustomed to be marryed. Att w[ch] tyme he well remembreth S[r] Frauncis Knowlles, father unto the Countesse, did give her for wief unto the aforenamed Erle of Leicester, in the sight and presence of this Deponent, the Erle of Pembrooke, the Lord North, S[r] Frauncis Knolles, M[r] Tindall, and Mr*

Richard Knowlles, all wch were present and saw the said mariage solemized, as he hath deposed."[5]

Leicester died on September 4th, 1588; an inventory was taken of all his property, real and personal, the original of which is now in the British Museum. From it it appears that the furniture, library, horses, etc., at Wanstead were valued at £1,119 6s. 6d. The pictures, among which were portraits of Henry VIII, Queen Mary and Elizabeth, and many others, not particularised, were valued at £11 13s. 4d. How different the value would be now, for these pictures were undoubtedly originals by the best masters.[6] The library consisted only of an old Bible, the Acts and Monuments, old and torn, seven psalters and a service book; they were valued at 13s. 8d. The horses were valued at £316 0s. 8d. The bill for the Earl's funeral amounted to the enormous sum of £4,000.

By his will Leicester appointed Wanstead House as a residence for his widow. The Countess Lettice was not long in consoling herself, for in less than twelve months she married her third husband, Sir Christopher Blount[xxxv]. Indeed, there were not wanting scandal-mongers to hint that the Countess poisoned No. 2 in order to marry No. 3, and when we remember the dark suspicion still attaching to the tragedy of Leicester's first Countess, we cannot but admit that stern justice would have been satisfied if his second Countess really had poisoned him.

Notwithstanding the fact that his personal estate was valued at £29,820, an enormous sum for those days, Leicester was in considerable debt to the Crown, and other creditors.

Lord Treasurer Burghley[xxxvi] writes on November 16th, 1593:

---

[5] State Papers, Domestic, Elizabeth, vol. 148, No. 24.

[6] A list of the pictures at Wanstead House is printed in *Notes and Queries,* 3rd series, vol. ii, p. 225. VOL. IX.

"Divers debts of the late Earl of Leicester due to Her Majesty remain still unpaid by Sir Christopher Blount and the Countess of Leicester, his wife, executrix of the said Earl; for satisfaction thereof, the manor of Wanstead stands extended, the inheritance of which has now, by lawful conveyance, come to the Earl of Essex. Sir Christopher Blount has desired that this manor may be exchanged for manors mentioned in the Counties of Warwick, Salop, Gloucester, and Middlesex, that she may be more speedily satisfied. He is to issue processes for the seizure of these manors, to discharge Wanstead, and to send particulars of the premises, for the demising thereof to the said Sir Christopher Blount and the Countess, during such seizure and extent."

This "lawful conveyance" to Essex must have been by Leicester's heirs, who at this date were his sister Katherine[xxxvii], wife of Henry Hastings, Earl of Huntingdon[xxxviii], and his great- niece Elizabeth Sidney[xxxix], daughter and heiress of Sir Philip, and wife of Roger Manners, Earl of Rutland[xl]. Sir Philip Sidney, as has already been mentioned, was the eldest son of Leicester's other sister, Mary, who married Sir Henry Sidney; he was killed at the siege of Zutphen in 1586. Neither the Countess of Huntingdon nor the Countess of Rutland left children, so that eventually Robert Sidney[xli], the second son of Sir Henry Sidney and Mary Dudley[xlii], became heir, and he was created Earl of Leicester in 1618.

The Earl of Essex[xliii], Robert Devereux, who now became owner of Wanstead, was the son of Lettice, Countess of Leicester, by her first husband. It looks as though the sale was the result of a family arrangement.

John Chamberlain[xliv] writes on August 30th, 1598:

"The Lord Treasurer's funeral [Lord Burghley's] was performed yesterday with all the rites that belonged to so great a personage. The number of mourners, one and other, were above 500, wherof there were many noble men, and among the rest the Erle of Essex, who (whether it were upon the consideration of the present occasion, or for his owne disfavours), methought, carried the heaviest countenance of the companie. Presently, after dinner, he retired to Wansted, where they say he meanes to settle, seing he cannot be received in Court,

9

though he have relented much, and sought by divers meanes to recover his hold. But the Quene sayes he hath plaide longe enough upon her, and that she meanes to play awhile upon him, and to stand as much upon her greatness as he hath done upon stomacke."

The same genial gossip, writing on March 15th, 1599, says:

" Lord Mountjoy has bought Wanstead of the Earl of Essex."

The date is significant, for Essex had just been appointed to the command of the army sent to Ireland to repress the rebellion of Hugh O'Neil, Earl of Tyrone[xlv]. The campaign was a miserable fiasco, and the Queen was naturally indignant. Essex hurried back to London to make peace with his Royal Mistress, and on his failure to do so, commenced a treasonable conspiracy, for which he was executed on February 25th, 1601.

CHARLES BLOUNT, Lord Mountjoy[xlvi], to which title he succeeded in 1594, the new owner of Wanstead, was a soldier of some distinction, and had seen a considerable amount of active service. He was present at the Battle of Zutphen[xlvii] in 1586, where Sir Philip Sidney received his fatal wound; he fitted out a ship at his own expense to join in pursuit of the Armada in 1588; he accompanied Essex on his voyage to the Azores in 1597, and on his return was made a Knight of the Garter.

In November, 1599, he succeeded Essex as Lord Deputy of Ireland, and after a lengthy campaign, Tyrone submitted on December 22nd, 1602. In the following May, Mountjoy returned to England, bringing Tyrone with him, and the victor and the vanquished lived together at Wanstead until August, when Tyrone was allowed to return to Ireland. In con-sideration of Mountjoy's successes in this matter, he was created Earl of Devonshire on July 21st, 1604. He died on April 3rd, 1606, at Savoy House[xlviii] in the Strand, and was buried in Westminster Abbey.

On December 3rd, 1605, the Earl had gone through a ceremony of marriage with Penelope[xlix], the divorced wife of Lord Rich[l], and sister of the Earl of Essex. He left no legitimate issue, and his titles became extinct. In 1604, February 10th, Lord Mountjoy, as he then was, had executed a settlement of all his estates, which were very numerous, and included the historic Castle of Fotheringhay. The Wanstead property is described as "the Lordshipps and Mannors of Wansteed and Stonehall, and the Parke commonly called Wansteed Parke, and the advowson of the Church and Rectory of Wainsted in the County of Essex." The whole was settled on his sons successively in tail, and, in default, as he should appoint by his will. The Earl, as already stated, had no legitimate children. By his will, dated April 2nd, 1606, the day before he died, the Earl gave nearly all his property, including Wanstead, to Thomas, Earl of Suffolk[li], and other trustees, for the life of "the Lady Penelope, one of the daughters of the late Right Honourable Walter, Earle of Essex, my very deare and loveing wife, upon especiall trust and confidence which I repose in their Lordshipps for and in behalf of the said Lady Penelope, who is hereby to have her chiefest maintenance and stay of livinge, most heartely beseeching their Lordshipps to accept of this estate for her good." After her death, "Sir Mountjoy Blount, alias Ryche, one of the sonnes of the said Lady Penelope," was to have the property, and the other sons and daughters of the Earl and Lady Penelope are named in succession; in default of all these Lady Penelope's own heirs were to take.

Lady Penelope did not long survive to enjoy her life estate, for she died at Westminster on July 6th, 1608, and the property passed under the Earl's will to his illegitimate son, Sir Mountjoy Blount[lii], who was created Baron Mountjoy in 1618, and Earl of Newport in 1628.

King James seems to have had a great affection for Wanstead, and visited it frequently. He could get to it easily from Greenwich by crossing the river, and it was conveniently near Theobalds, his favourite house in Hertfordshire. Nicholls, in his Progresses of James I[liii], records many occasions on which James was at Wanstead, but as most of these notes do not throw any light on the history of the place, only a selection are printed here.

The first of these visits was in September, 1607; "The King's Majesty hath beene here at Tibbolles and Wanstead since his return from the Western Progress, and removes not hence till Munday to Whitehall, and Tuesday to Hampton Court, where the Queene is." This was after the Earl of

11

Devonshire's death and before Lady Penelope's; it would have been interesting to learn who was the host or hostess on the occasion. It can hardly have been Lady Penelope herself, for the Court had refused to receive her after her divorce from Lord Rich. The house may have been let, as it certainly was a few years later.

On September 11th, 1611, Sir Roger Aston[liv] writes "from Wenssted" to Lord Salisbury[lv]: "I send yor L. here in closed his Mat[s] letter to the K. of Denmarke[lvi]; his plesoure is yo[r] L. shall cause it to be coppeed and seled, and derected this day. His Ma[ty] keld a stag, and derected that it mough [might] be presently sentt to yo[r] L. to send to Docter Jonas[lvii]."

In 1612, James was again at Wanstead. John Chamberlain, writing on June 17th to Sir Dudley Carleton[lviii], says:-"The King hath been coming and going to Eltham all the last week. He went thither on Saturday and came back on Monday; and yesterday went thither again, and is this night to lie at Wanstead, which house the Master of the Rolls hath taken, and entertained him there, with the charge, it is said, of £700."

The Master of the Rolls here referred to was Sir Edward Phellips[lix], so appointed in 1611, Speaker of the House of Commons from 1604 to 1611. He had already built the beautiful manor house at Montacute, in Somerset (still standing, and still owned by the Judge's descendants), and Wanstead was probably only rented by him.

The house had apparently not a very good reputation for healthiness. The Earl of Northampton[lx] writes to Viscount Rochester[lxi], on August 17th, 1612: "I beseech yo[r] Lo. that the state of thinges at Wanstedd may be well considered and examined before the K[ing] come thether ; for we saw that very many have bine dangerously sick, and one deade at the laste, which proves that the place is in no very good plight for such a Kinge to resort unto."

On December 20th, 1617, Chamberlain writes to Carleton :- "Younge Blount, Rich, or Montjoy, heyre to the Earle of Devonshire, is shortly to be made a Baron, for the w[ch] he parts wth the house and land at Wansted, but whether to the K. or Earle of Buckingham[lxii] I know not." Buckingham was

12

the recipient of this handsome bribe, and Blount duly got his Barony, being created Baron Mountjoy on January 31st, 1618.

In 1627 Lord Mountjoy married Anne, daughter of John, Lord Butler[lxiii]. Her mother, Elizabeth, was a daughter of Sir George Villiers of Brokesby, Leicestershire, and a half-sister of Buckingham's, which perhaps accounts for the fact that Mountjoy was created Earl of Newport in 1628. He died on February 12th, 1666, and was buried in Christ Church, Oxford.

In 1630, as we shall see later, he tried to regain Wanstead, on the ground that he was a minor when he parted with it.

George Villiers, afterwards Duke of Buckingham, the new owner of Wanstead, like Leicester, seemed to fill the period of history in which he lived. The younger son of a Leicestershire gentleman, he succeeded, by his good looks and courtly manners, in captivating not only James, but later on his son and successor, Charles I[lxiv]. No romance writer of the times can let Buckingham alone, and even the French writers (notably Alexandre Dumas) have wrapped him up in a halo of glory, which certainly he did not deserve. His assassination, by Felton, relieved England of one of the most profligate, contemptible, and base Court favourites that it has ever suffered from. Handsome in person, with a superficial grace obtained at the French Court, he was mean and treacherous, and particularly so in relation to women.

His rise was phenomenal. Born in 1592, he was created a Knight of the Garter in 1616, Viscount Villiers in the same year, Earl of Buckingham in 1617, Marquis of Buckingham in 1618, and Duke of Buckingham in 1623. He was assassinated on August 23rd, 1628, and was buried in Westminster Abbey.

On June 26th, 1618, Camden records in his Annals that the King was entertained most splendidly by the Marquis of Buckingham at Wanstead House, which he is said to have then presented to the King. Rumour was wrong this time, for Buckingham did not give his property away.

The King was again at Wanstead in July, and while there (on the 11th) the Letters Patent creating Sir Francis Bacon[lxv], the Lord Chancellor, Baron of Verulam, were sealed.

Buckingham did not retain Wanstead very long, for he sold it early in 1619 to Sir Henry Mildmay[lxvi].

On June 19th, 1619, Chamberlain writes:-"The King came unlooked for from Theobalds to Whitehall on Thursday. He went hence yesterday morning very early to Theobalds, and at night was entertained by young Sir Henry Mildmay at Wanstead, which he hath lately purchased of the Marquis of Buckingham."

Sir Henry Mildmay, the purchaser of Wanstead, was the second son of Humphrey Mildmay of Danbury, Essex, and grandson of Sir Walter Mildmay of Apthorpe, Northants, Chancellor of the Exchequer, and Founder of Emmanuel College, Cambridge, by Mary, sister of Sir Francis Walsingham[lxvii]. He was knighted in 1617, being then one of the King's Sewers or servers. In April, 1619, he married Anne, one of the daughters and, eventually, co-heirs of Sir William Halliday[lxviii], a wealthy Alderman of London, and Governor of the East India Company[lxix]; it is said that the King gave him two manors, worth £12,000, to make his estate somewhat proportionate to his wife's. Wanstead may perhaps have been one of these, or Mildmay may have bought it out of part of his wife's fortune. He was appointed Master of the King's Jewel House in April, 1620. Notwithstanding many royal favours, he sided with the Parliament against Charles I, though he does not appear to have done much fighting in the Civil War. He was nominated one of King Charles's judges, and attended the trial on January 23rd, 25th, and 26th, 1649, but abstained from signing the death warrant. Some notes on his trial and sentence as one of the Regicides[lxx], will appear later.

King James continued to visit the new owner almost as frequently as he did Buckingham, and we find notes of his being at Wanstead in July and September, 1619; June and September, 1620; June, 1621; June and July, 1622; June, July, and September, 1623; and June and July, 1624. Most of these do not call for further mention, but a few will appear in due course.

14

About this time there was a project of making Wanstead a rival to Tunbridge Wells, owing to the discovery of a spring of mineral water. Chamberlain writes to Carleton on August 23rd, 1619:

> *"We have great noise here [London] of a new Spaa or spring of that nature, found lately about Wansted, and much running there is to yt dayly, both by Lords and Ladies and other great companie, so that they have almost drawne yt drie alredy ; and yf yt shold hold on, yt wold put downe the waters at Tunbridge, wch for these three or fowre yeares have ben much frequented, specially this summer by many great persons, insomuch that they wch have seene both say yt is not inferior to the spaa for good companie, number of people, and other appurtenances."*

The friendly interest taken by James I in the young Knight and his wife is shown by the following letter written by Mr. Secretary Conway[lxxi] (afterwards Viscount Conway) to the Attorney General.

> *"21 Aug., 1623. "S^r -His Matie is informed of the great indisposicion in health of Sr William Holladay, Governor of the East India Companie ; for wch his Matie is exceedinge sorrie, in regard hee was a verie worthie and well deservinge Magistrate and Minister to him. And because his Matie understandeth that you have speciall intrest in Sr William Holladay, Hee is graciously pleased to recommend unto yor favour his servaunt Sr Henrie Mildmay, and prayes you to doe him the best offices you can for his advantage in that estate hee is to receave by his wife, and that hee doe not suffer anie prejudice therein. This his Matie will take well, and thank you for."*

Chamberlain, writing on June 19th, 1624, says:

> *"This is the K's birth day, wch he kepes at Wansted, and will tary there till Wensday : he went a hunting early this morning wth the Countesse of Buckingam and her daughter Denbigh, on horsbacke."*

Mildmay wrote to Lord Conway on October 28th, 1625:

"I cannot omitt the giveinge your Lordeship all due and homble thankes for that good and noble office you did me to the Duke by your Letters, assureinge you whot grouth I shall have in his favour shall be honestly imploied to doe you faithfull service move not from Wonsteede untill I heere from your Lordeship. . . . Thus desiringe to be preserved still in your favor in the name of Your Lordeships faithful servant,

HENRY MILDEMAY."

The nature of the "good and noble office" does not appear; the Duke was doubtless Buckingham.

King Charles I does not appear to have been quite so fond of Wanstead as his father was, but several visits are recorded. He was there three times in 1627, in June, July, and September; in August, 1628; and in September, 1630. The second of these visits is referred to in the two following documents.

Sir Robert Heath, the Attorney General, to Sir Francis Nethersall, July 11th, 1627:

"I have receaved yor lett^r. Yo^r servaunt the last day did tell me the formr day was put of, but left me word that I herd of what indeed was appointed. I would very gladly have attended this afternoon, to give you satisfaction. But it soe falls out I cann not possibly. I am commaunded by the king to attend him at Wansted this afternoon, wth S^r Th. Fanchaue, for directions about the king's service ..... Thus intreating you to excuse me out of this necessitye, I rest, Your very loving frend readye to serve you, Ro. HEATH."

The King signed the following warrant at Wanstead, on July 13th, 1627.

"CHARLES.

Our will and pleasure is that instantly vpon sight hereof you put yo'self and our ship vnder yor command in readinesse with the first wind to transport this bearer, Mr Walter Montague, and such as shall goe with

16

him, vnto some convenient port of the Vnited Provinces, And having landed him, to repaire either to Flushing or Groll and there attend and follow such directions as you shall there receive from Our Ambassador, the Lord Carleton, to whome you are to give knowledge with all speed you can of yo[r] arrivall in those parts. And this shall bee yo[r] warrant. Given at our Court at Wanstead, 13 July, the third yeare of o[r] raigne.

To o[r] trustie and wellbeloved Francis Sidenham, Capt[n] of our good ship called The Marie Rose."

In January, 1629, we get an incidental mention of Wanstead in a letter referring to some lawless doings in the neighbourhood.

The Earl of Totnes to Viscount Conway, Lord President of the Council :

"My very Good Lord

This inclosed letter I received this morninge from Sir Nicholas Coote[lxxii], a Justice of Peace in Essex, dwellinge neare vnto Wanstead, in the Forrest. I would have wayted vpon you my self, but this Colde weather enforceth me to stay in my howse. I make no dowbt but you will take it into yo[r] Consideration, and in yo[r] wisdome acquainte the Lords of His Ma[ties] Counsell with the same, that p[r]sent order may be taken, for the repressinge of the Insolencyes now in the budd, before they growe to farther strength. Savoy, the 27th of Jan., 1628" [i. e. 1628-9].

The inclosed letter from Sir Nicholas Coote is dated at Wyfields, January 27th, 1629. It reports various cases of highway robberies, men and women carrying off corn intended for export, swearing they would first provide for themselves, with tumults consequent thereon.

In September, 1630, Charles was again at Wanstead, and there he signed the two next documents.

"CHARLES R.

Our will and pleasure is, That you forthwth drawe vpp and prepare a Booke fitt for o^r Royall signature Conteyninge o^r Gratious and Free Pardon vnto William Sneade For his killinge of one Edward Worthington aboute Nyneteene yeares past, In as ample and benificiall wise to that purpose, As yo^u have heretofore done, And for soe doinge this shalbe yor sufficient Warrant. Given at o^r Courte at Wansted, the nynth of September in the sixt yeare of o^r Raygne.

To or Trustie and welbeloved Sr Robert Heath, Knight, our Attorney Generall, or Sr Richard Shelton Knight, our Sollicito1 generall, or to eyther of them."

"CHARLES R.

Right reverend father in God right trustie and Wellbeloved, We greet you well. We understand by the humble petition of our trustie and wellbeloved Andrew Bird, Schoolemaster of our free scoole in the Borrough of Reading, presented vnto us with the consent of the Mayo^r and Burgesses, that whereas through the speciall favor and bountie of our predecesso^{rs} the Inhabitants of our said Bourrough have long enjoyed the benefit of one publick and free scoole without the molestacion or interruption of any other attempting to teach Grammar in the towne, but such onely as have beene tolerated to initiate and prepare children for that publicke schoole, Yet of late there hath beene a licence granted by yor Chancellor vnto one to teach Grammar there, which for the present doth tend much to the prejudice of the said bourrough and schoole, and the continuance thereof may be a meanes in short time utterly to decay the same. For prevencion hereof both now and hereafter Wee have thought it fit (according to the humble suite made unto us in that behalf) hereby to make knowne unto you that our pleasure, that you presently cause the said licence obtained from your Chancello^r to bee revoked, and that no such licence bee graunted hereafter to any other which may occasion the decay of our said schoole and deprive our said bourrough of the benefit which they enjoye thereby. Given vnder o^r Signet at o^r Court at Wansted, the 10 day of 7^{ber} In the 6 yeare of o^r raigne."

In 1630 Lord Newport made the effort to recover Wanstead, already referred to [p. 171]. Instead of commencing proceedings at law or in equity, he, acting presumably on legal advice, presented a petition to the King, setting out the facts on which he relied.

" To the Kinge's Most Excellent Matie. The humble peticion of yor humblest servant, Mountioy, Earle of Newport.

Sheweth, that hee (having for divers yeares of late been employed in yor Ma^ts service abroad, wch hath been expencefull unto him, and during that tyme wanting opportunity to look into his owne estate ; now lately retireing himselfe; findeth the meanes left to him by his father to be wasted neere unto the one halfe. And in particuler the Manno^r of Wansted, a large portion of his bequeathed Revennue, the only convenient habitacion left unto him, and by his father's will specially exempted from sale, to be conveyed away dureing his minority, w^thout one penny recompence to him for it, or any other advantage in regard thereof; Notw^thstanding a Rent charge of 200li. per annum by his father laid upon those Lands hath ever since byn paid by him. This Conveyance he conceiveth is defective, and he hopeth in a legall course he may recover it agayne. Now his humble sute unto yor Maty is only this, that as a Subject he may have the benefitt of yor Lawes, and that the present possesso^r thereof be left to his just defence in Lawe or equity ; The rather because he beleeveth that the purchaser paid in true estimacion little; sure hee is [that] nothing att all was paid to him, or to his benefitt. And yor Pet^r shall ever pray for yor Ma^ts long and prosperous Raigne."

The result of this petition does not appear, but apparently it was unsuccessful so far as the recovery of Wanstead was concerned. Lord Newport, however, seems to have had a "consolation prize" to make up for his disappointment, for in June, 1630, a warrant was issued for granting the custody of Hyde Park, co. Middlesex, to Mountjoy, Earl of Newport, and Sir John Smith[lxxiii], to take effect after death of Henry, Earl of

19

Holland[lxxiv], or the surrender of his grant. It seems difficult to believe that this grant was not in some way connected with the fruitless petition as to Wanstead.

CONTINUING our extracts from the State Papers, the next document is a letter written at Wanstead by Sir Henry Mildmay to Viscount Dorchester :

My Lorde,

Whereas about the time of Lente laste paste your Lordship did answere a petition of one Captaine Dimes by his Maties direction to the Master and Courte of Wardes, that the saide Captain shoulde have the gardenship of one Doctor Bankeworth and his estate, yf he proved to be a Lunituicke. Upon wch the Master of that Corte attended his Ma^ty, and acquainted him that by the lawes of the relme noe proffit ought to be made of any Lunatick's estate, and that his Ma^ty had only the protection of such, and that my selfe

VOL. X. 64

beinge a very neere neighbor to the Doctor, out of a care to keepe him out of daungerous handes, was the first that did petition the Corte of Wardes for the Gardenship of him and his estate, and that it coulde not be graunted from me w^thout much disgrace and wronge to me, and allsoe wthout breatch of his Maties instructions to that Corte, that he that first petitions, beinge a man able to be answerable for his estate, shall have him yf he be not nexte a kin ; wherevpon his Ma^tys answere to the Master of that Corte was that the Captain shoulde then looke out for somewbot els.

Nowe (my Lorde) in regarde that I heere an intention in some to move his Ma^ty to have the Custody of him and his estate, I intreate you to put his Ma^ty in minde of his former answere to the Master of the Wardes, and I am confident his Ma^ty will not give way to any thing to my prejudice in this, my desire beinge only out of charrity as a neighbor, and allsoe beinge moved by his neerest freindes to take upon me the gardenship of him and his estate to protect boath. Thus much I hombly intreat your Lordeship, by way of prevention, to doe for him that is at

Your Lordship's service to commande,

Henry: Mildmay.

Wonsteede, August [6th], 1631.

To the right honor^ble my Lorde Vicount Dorchister, Principall Secretary of Estate.

There was an outbreak of the plague in London in 1636, and the King therefore proposed to spend the summer out of town. As a precautionary measure, the following letter was sent by the Privy Council to the Justices of the Peace near Oatlands, Hampton Court, Havering and Wanstead, and to the Bailiffs of Kingston on Thames.

Whereas Wee vnderstand that by reason of the Infeccion in and neere London, multitudes of Tradesmen and others flying into the Country Tounes doe there inhabite 2 or 3 families Inmates in one house ; wch is not only contrary to lawe, but in this tyme of Contagion may proove very dangerous to such Tounes and the Country adjoyning. And whereas his Matie Intends to be at Havering Parke and Wanstead oftentymes this Sommer, [Their Ma^tes doe intend to reside at Hampton Courte and at Oatelands most of this summer. Marginal note.] Wee have therefore thought good in his Maties name straitely to charge and command you, wthin yor severall devicions, strictly to enquire and examine what houses in that Countie w^thin 10 miles of Havering or Wanstead doe receive severall Famelies as Inmates or sojurners [or are otherwise pestered with lodgers. Struck out.] And to take effectuall and speadie order for the present removeing of them and reformeing of abuses in this kinde, and punishing such as contrary to lawe have or shall receive and harber them, whereby to prevent the danger of

21

Infeccion that may otherwise be brought thether by such disorder. And thus, not doubting of yor care and best endevors in a service so much importing the safetie of his Maties person, and the lives of his subjects, Wee bid you, &c. Dated the 19th of June, 1636.

(Signed)

Lo. Keeper	*Ea. Sterline*	*Lo. Cottington*
Lo. Privie Seale	*Lo. V. Wimbledon*	*Mr. Sec. Coke*
Ea. of Holland	*Lo. V. Wentworth*	*Mr. Sec'. Windebanke*

[Endorsed.] 19 June, 1636. A minute for 4 letters to be written for removing of Inmates, &c, from inhabitating neare his Maties houses in this time of Contagion.

The following letters relate to the collection of Ship Money.[lxxv]

1636, July 9. Sir Humphrey Mildmay to Secretary Nicholas[lxxvi].

MR. NICHOLAS,

This letter heere Inclosed from one of the Highe Constables of Onger Hundred. The Contents I pray cause to be read on Sonday Nexte, before the Lords. I was att Eppinge on Friday in the Whittson Weeke, the Constables of Hundreds wth me; att that day I made this Rate Inclosed for Stanford Rivers, wth the good Consente of M^r. William Petre, made John Glascocke of Morreton, and Thomas Sumpner, Collecto^rs, both of them beinge riche men, and Principall Inhabbitaunts of the sameParrishe ; their answere you may see by the Highe Constable. I hope the Lords will Considder of me in this Sullen answere of theres, and will have them both Convented before their Lo. I must much commende the Highe Constable, whoe hath bene very forewarde and aydeing unto me, and hath payde me the greateste partes of the Monny of his parte. I wishe his fellowe had donne the like, and then I shoulde be the nearer to my Jorneyes Eande. In that Hundred Mr Petre hath longe and much Complained of the backwardenes of his

22

Neighbours In this Servis, whoe hath bene allwayes ready and willinge todoe his parte. Yf it please the Lordes to call for these fellowes, I will not be idle, but will Leavy 31l. of their goods. Lett them smarte well, for they are in the galle of Mallis towards the Servis. To answere the letter from the borde, I doe not believe that there is 3,100l. behinde in the County of Essex. You knowe that I have pᵈ 1,400l. and have 600l. att home ready to paye ; that the Towne of Colchester hath 400l., all this beinge pᵈ in

2,400l., and to emagine that there is 2,000l. more to gather, is more then I dare presume of. I will doe the uttermost of my Duety to bringe inn all behinds, and what I finde I will trewly paye wᵗʰout fraude, and doe hope that there Lo. will thinke that I doe what I am able, by peece and peece, for I proteste there is noe penny pd that is not forced ; god helpe me amongeste the people yf there Lo. favor me not. I have shewed there Lo. letters to Sʳ Cran. Harris, whoe hathe a Coppye thereof. One worde more. I doubte not but that I shall bringe inn all the Monny behinds, wᵗʰ their Lo. favor and helpe, in tyme when I shall require it, as I shall Complaine in cases of moste Importance. And wᵗʰ my Servis I am and reste, by you to be comaunded, Wanstead this 9ᵒ Jul., Aᵒ 1636.

H. MILDMAY.

To the Right worᴵᴵ and his very Loveing friend, Mʳ. Nicholas, one of his Maties Clarkes of the Privie Councell.

1636, July 9th. Sir Henry Mildmay to Secretary Nicholas.

MR. NICKLAS,

Vpon tusday last, whilest my Brother the Highchreife of Essex came up to attende my Lorde Thresurar, he sente the Baily of the Hundared of Onger and this yonge man, his servant, to receave some of his Matys monnies due at a towne caled Stamford rivers, the hole towne beinge a very great parrish haveinge paide noe penny of the Shipmdney, except one, wᶜʰ I impute rather to be the faulte of the Collectors there, the perticcular inhabbitants wthin that parrish; the carridge of one of the Collectors boath in refusinge to be collector and rescuinge his catle by force out of the hands of the Baily of the hundard, haveinge a warrant from the Highchreife, I leave to this man's relation, together wth his ill wordes; but I perceave many in those partes make a stop of payinge untill they heere whot becomes of this Collector. My Brother beinge nowe at the other ende of the cuntary, dilligent in his Ma^{tys}. service, I thought fit to write to you to acquaint my Lordes wth the true state of his busines, wch is of importance, that this fellowe, whoe in other services hath beene refractary, may be punnished accordinge to his demerret, for I perceave as this man speades it will either further or retarde his Ma^{tys} service in those partes; wch I thought fittinge to acquaint you before my Brother proceede against him, accordinge to that authority wch he hath, that he may receave theire Lordships directions, whch he shall immediatly performe.

The nuse of this busines came to me by my Brothers man, to Wonsted, this Satterday, beinge the 9 of July, at 4 of the clock afternoons.

Your assured loveinde freinde,

HENRY MILDMAY.

To his very worthy good friend Mr Nicholas, or in his absence to any of the rest of the Clarkes of his Ma^{ts} most hono^{ll} Privie Councell, now attending att the Court att Otelandes.

1636, November 17. Sir Humphrey Mildmay to the Privy Council.

May it please your Lordshippes: That on friday laste, beinge the 11th of Novembre, I sawe by accident that letter to the nowe Sherriffe of Essex and that postscripte that concerned me, the late Sherriffe ; and since that, on Monday laste, beinge the 14th of the same Moneth, beinge on the waye towardes Sr William Russell, I had deliverd vnto me a letter by one of the Messengers, of the 7th of this November in Windsor. The Contents are, vnder your Lo. favour, as I doe Conceyve, that I shoulde gather upp all such sommes and arreres as are behinde in the County of Essex, and farther that I shoulde Certefye ypur Lo. and the bordes what are the Causes and delayes that his Ma. Monny hath not beine payde in soe longe a tyme. Nowe may it farther please your Lo. to knowe that beinge the County is very lardge and that I coulde not possibly attende in all places, I made Schedules to the Balleiffes of Hundreds of all the defaulters in every devision, Parrishe and Hamblett, in soe plaine a manner that he or they could not Ignorantely erre in such a servis, yf they had pleased. And att the laste Quarter Sessions wch was after Michelmas, the Balleiffes beinge all there attendinge, and Callinge them to Accoumpte howe they had proceeded, I founde Manny of them soe false that they had not soe much as demaunded those Somes att all; yett nott with- standinge I employed some men of my owne, that did bringe inn some Monny to make vpp my last payemente. And wheras your Lo. Comaundes me to give the names of all such as have not payde or have beine distreyned, the bulke woulde be very greate, yett under favour I doe Conceive that youre Lo. Meaneinges are of those beinge of ranke and Quallety, the wch are not Manny, and such as I doubte not but beinge in the presence of any one of your Lo. woulde be perswaded to such reasons as your Lo. shoulde require of them ; but yf I may offer to intreate that a reformation may be had vppon some of the Cheefe Constables, some untowarde Londoners and the Bayleiffes, I doe conceyve, under favour, that the worke that your Lo. Comaundes me to doe woulde be very easie, and woulde render such exsample and terror, that the evill affected woulde quake att the noise thereof, And his Ma. Monny woulde come in roundely. I have made boulde to drawe a shorte Schedule of the Names and places of such as I knowe have beine untowarde in this Servis, And such as I doubte not but your Lo. will finde (beinge examined) to be Agreeable to what I write of them. All wh^{ch} I humbly submitt to your Lo. Considerations, And doe most humblie intreate that youre Lo. wilbe pleased to Move his Ma. that In regarde of my Meane Estate, greate Chardge, and the Intollerable paines and labours that I have taken, both in boddie and Minde, in this servis, that I may be spared and May resigne both My Accoumptes to the nowe Sherriffe, wth all such papers as doeth Concerne this Servis. And I shalbe ever bounde in *all dewtie to Blesse his Ma. and your Lo. And wth pardon for my sadenes, I doe Crave pardon and remaine to be*

Youre Lo. Humble servaunte,

17º November, Aº 1636. In Wanstead.

H. MILDMAY.

To the Right Honnorable the Lordes of his Ma. Moste Hon. Privye Councell.

1638, July 11. Sir Henry Mildmay to Secretary Nicholas.

MR. NICHOLAS,

I thanke you verie much for lettinge me see the order made by the Lordes before yʳ hand went to it. But wheras it is written to search from Hen. 8, may you please (yf you may) with yr penn to put that out, and write, to search from the first of Queen Elizabeth, you shall exceedinglie obleige me; however, yf you can not doe it so, I leave it to you as you thinke best, and shalbe readie ever to approve my selfe

Your assured, true freinde,

Wonsted, July 11, 1638.

HENRY MILDMAY.

To his worthy good freinde, Mr Nicholas, Clarke of the Councell of Estate, neere Eggam, these.

ON the Restoration of Charles II[lxxvii] a Committee was appointed to make preparations for the Coronation. On May 15th, 1660, the House of Commons ordered "that Sir Henry Mildmay, Mr. Cornelius Holland[lxxviii], and Mr. Nicholas Love[lxxix], do forthwith attend the Committee to whom it is referred to consider of Requisites for his Majesty's Reception, to give an account of what is become of the Crown, Robes, Sceptre, and Jewels, belonging to the King's Majesty[lxxx]."

Whatever became of the crown (Sherlock Holmes, it will be remembered, thought that he had found it hidden in an old manor house) there is no doubt that a very large amount of the late King's property had disappeared.

Somewhat later, on August 14th, 1660, a Proclamation was published "for restoring and discovering his Majesties goods, plate, jewels, houshold-stuff, cabinets, statues, inscriptions, pictures, drawings, sculptures, rings, stones, ancient coyns, medalls, books, manuscripts, peices of art, etc., which did belong to our late dear Father, our Mother the Queen, or to our Selfe, which have been purloyn'd and embezilled."

Much of this was no doubt in Mildmay's official custody, and he was openly charged with peculation. He had no stomach for any investigation, and determined to escape to the continent. He got as far as Rye, but before he could find a vessel to take him to France, he was discovered and arrested on May 17th. He was at once sent to Dover Castle, where he remained in confinement for some weeks.

Meanwhile the Commons had resolved (May 17th) that all persons who sat in judgment upon the late King's Majesty, when sentence of Death was pronounced against him, and the estates both real and personal of all and every the said persona whether in their own hands or otherwise, should be forthwith seized and secured ; and all ports were to be stopped, so that none should escape.

On June 9th following, the Commons resolved, "That Sir Henry Mildmay, Knight, be excepted out of the Act of General Pardon and Oblivion, for and in respect only of such Pains, Penalties and Forfeitures (not extending to Life) as shall be thought fit to be inflicted on him by another Act, intended to be hereafter passed for that purpose." And also "That Sir Henry Mildmay, now Prisoner at Dover, be sent up in custody from Dover, and committed Prisoner to the Tower of London: And the Lieutenant of Dover Castle be, and hereby is, required to send him up in custody to the Tower accordingly."

On June 18th, the humble Petition of Sir Henry Mildmay Knight, was read in the House of Commons. It was ordered that his commitment to the

Tower be suspended, and that he be forthwith committed to the charge and custody of the Serjeant-at-Arms attending this House. On August 6th he was apparently released on finding good security; but on the 24th he was recommitted to the Tower.

On July 21st, 1661, Mildmay was brought to the Bar of the House of Lords, and having kneeled as a Delinquent, the Speaker told him that a Bill was brought up from the House of Commons, which proposed that he should forfeit all his lands and goods and undergo certain pains and penalties, "for sitting in that traiterous pretended High Court of Justice whereby his late Majesty was sentenced to be murdered," and demanded if he had anything to say why the Bill should not pass.

Sir Henry confessed that he sat once in that Court[7], and no more, and was heartily sorry for the same, and begged for mercy.

The sentence which had been pronounced against him was that he should be degraded from all honours and titles, and every year on the anniversary of the sentence on Charles I, January 27th, he should be drawn upon a sledge through the streets to and under the gallows at Tyburn, with a rope round his neck, and so back to the Tower, there to remain a prisoner for life.

He presented the following petition :-

To the right hon^ble the Lords in Parliament assembled.

The humble petition of Sr Henry Mildmay,

In all humility sheweth:

That yor pet^r, being most deepely sensible of ye just displeasure of ye honble House of Commons declared against hym and others in the Bill there latelie passed for paines, penalties and forfeitures, and now depending before yor Lo^pps, the offence therein charged against him

---

[7] As to Sir Henry's sittings, see *ante*, p. 77.

being for sitting and acting in that prtended high Court of justice for trying and judging of his late Matie of blessed memorie. The onlie end wch your pet^{r} proposed to hymselfe for appearing in that pretended court, was, that hee might by his being there prsent, and observing of theire proceedings, bee the better able to improve his utmost care and industry according to his allegeance, and special dutie to His late Ma^{ty} to preserve His said Maties life, wch yor pet^{r} endeavored wth all his diligence; and then also did (as hee now doeth), in the sinceritie of his heart, declare his utter abhorrencie and detestacion of that most wicked murther of His late Matie.

And inasmuch as the suddennes of yor pet^{rs} last appearing before the hon^{ble} House of Commons was such that hee had not then tyme to make proofe there of this his allegation ;

His most humble prayer therefore to yor Lo^{pps} now is that before the said Bill bee passed yor Lopps most honble House, yor pet^{r} may have liberty to produce his testimony to yor Lo^{pps} for cleering soe much of ye integrity of his intentions, wh^{ch} however it may weigh with yor good Lo^{pps}, hee shall humbly submitt to yor righteous judgment; Beseeching yor Lo^{pps} in ye bowells of yor compassion to him and his distressed children to commiserate his sad condition.

And (as in duty bound) hee shall, &c.

HENRY MILDMAY.

With this he sent a certificate from Dr. E. Warner that he was suffering from a rupture, and that if the sentence of drawing him in a sledge from the Tower to Tyburn were put in execution, it would endanger his life. Notwithstanding this, the sentence, so far as it related to his conveyance to Tyburn, was, according to Noble's *History of the Regicides*, solemnly carried out on January 30th, 1662.

In 1664 the sentence was relaxed as regards his imprisonment, and he was banished to Tangiers. The accounts of his death vary; one story states that he died at Antwerp, but Pepys[lxxxi] says that he died at Wanstead, as we shall see later. The Wanstead Parish Registers are not extant for this period, so that we cannot say if he was buried there or not. A very curious picture of Sir Henry lying dead in his bed is still in possession of the family.

The Act of Parliament above referred to [13 Charles II, chapter 15], mentions Mildmay by name. The title runs:-

> *"An Act declaring the Pains, Penalties and Forfeitures imposed upon the Estates and Persons of certaine notorious Offenders excepted out of the Act of Free and Generall Pardon, Indemptnity and Oblivion."*

After reciting the former act [12 Car. II, c. 11], it continues:-

> *" Wee therefore the Lords and Commons in Parliament assembled doe beseech your Majestie that it may be enacted and be it enacted. That all and every the Mannors, Messuages [etc.] of them the said .... Sir Henry Mildmay [and 26 others] which they or any of them or any other person or persons to their or any of their uses or in trust for them or any of them, had the five and twentieth day of March, 1646, or att any time since, shall stand and be forfeited unto, your Majesty, your Heires and Successors, and shall be deemed vested and adjudged to be in the actuall and reall possession of your Majestie without any Office or Inquisicion thereof hereafter to be taken or found."*

All goods, debts, and other chattels personal were also declared forfeited to the King. Bond-fide purchasers for valuable consideration were protected, but not the wives, children, or heirs of the offenders.

Wanstead accordingly became forfeited, and vested in the Crown by virtue of this Act. Morant states: "It is commonly said that his son, Henry Mildmay of Shawford in Hampshire, Esq., had divers suits to recover it, because it was settled on his mother, who was not guilty of treason; but as it was not her paternal estate, and only a settlement of his father's, it was forfeited, and could not be recovered." Noble says that some of Mildmay's estates, which had been settled in jointure, descended to his posterity.

King Charles II was especially requested to make provision for his brother out of these forfeited estates. Accordingly, on September 6th, 1661, Letters Patent were granted to John, Lord Berkley, Sir Charles Berkley junior, Knt, and Henry Brounkard, Esq., on the nomination of James, Duke of York[lxxxii], of all the lands and tenements late of Oliver Cromwell, Henry Ireton, John Bradshaw, Thomas Pride, and others (named) and of any other traitors attainted of high treason, granted to the King by any Act of Parliament; (Sir Henry Mildmay is not named specifically); To hold to them, their heirs and assigns, in free and common socage, and not in chief or by knight service, of the Manor of East Greenwich.[8]

It is somewhat remarkable that Mildmay is not named in this grant, but as he was one of "the other traitors attainted of High Treason," no doubt that covered his property sufficiently.

The Duke of York retained Wanstead exactly three months. On December 5th, 1661, he sold it to Sir Robert Brookes[lxxxiii], as appears by the following deed.

Indenture made December 5th, 1661. James, Duke of York, John, Lord Berckley of Stratton[lxxxiv], the Hon. Henry Brunckard[lxxxv] and Sir Charles Berckley[lxxxvi] the younger, Knight, the trustees mentioned in the previous grant, conveyed to Sir Robert Brookes of Cockfield Hall in Yoxford, Suffolk, Knight, in consideration of £3,500 to the Duke, and of £3,500 to the Duke and the trustees, and of 12d. apiece, "all those the Mannors and Lordshipps of Wanstead and Stonehall with the appurtenaunces in the County of Essex, and all that the capitall mesuage and house of Wanstead aforesaid and the Parke called or knowne by the name of Wanstead Parke, and also the advowson of the Church of Wanstead aforesaid," and all messuages, lands, etc., belonging thereto, including the great pond in the waste, called "Aldersbrooke Pond," and all appertenances in Wanstead, Walthamstow, Ilford, Barking, Woodford and "Laton," or in any other

---

[8] Patent Roll, 13 Charles II, part 25, no. 12.

town or parish in Essex, " heretofore knowne, used, taken or reputed to be the estate of Sir Henry Mildmay."[9]

Sir Robert Brookes held the manor until 1667. He afterwards retired to France, and died there in bad circumstances; some folk say murdered, for his body was found in the river at Lyons.

Pepys, in his Diary, gives us several stray notes on Wanstead. Writing on May 14th, 1665, he says: "To church it being Whit Sunday, my wife very fine in a new yellow bird's-eye hood, as the fashion is now. ... I took a coach and to Wanstead, the house where Sir Henry Mildmay died, and now Sir Robert Brookes lives, having bought it of the Duke York, it being forfeited to him. A fine seat, but an old-fashioned house, and being not full of people, looks flatly."

"1667, April 19th. Some talk of Sir W. Pen's being to buy Wansted House of Sir Robert Brookes; and I dare be hanged if ever he could mean to buy that great house, that knows not how to furnish one that is not the tenth part so big."

"1667, May 1st. Sir W. Penn[lxxxvii] did give me an account this afternoon of his design of buying Sir Robert Brookes's fine house at Wansted ; which I so wondered at, and did give him reasons against it, which he allowed of, and told me that he did intend to pull down the house and build a less, and that he should get £1,500 by the old house, and I know not what fooleries. But I will never believe he ever intended to buy it, for my part, though he troubled Mr. Gauden to go and look upon it and advise him in it."

Sir W. Penn here referred to was the father of the founder of Pennsylvania.

At this point we reach an important phase in the history of Wanstead.

In 1667, Sir Josiah Child[lxxxviii] became the purchaser of the manor of Wanstead, which at that time was estimated to be worth £1,000 a year, a

---

[9] Close Roll, 13 Charles II, part 4, no. 17.

decided increase on its value of forty shillings at the time of the Domesday Survey. He was the second son of Richard Child, a merchant, and was born in London in 1630. He commenced life as a merchant's apprentice, and accumulated a large fortune. He was a Director and afterwards Chairman of the East India Company, while his brother, Sir John[lxxxix], was Governor of Bombay. These two brothers are frequently confused with Francis Child[xc], the famous banker, but it is not certain that there was any relationship between the two families. At any rate, Sir Josiah had nothing to do with the bank still carried on at No. 1 Fleet Street, and the bankers had nothing to do with Wanstead.

John Evelyn[xci] of Wootton, the author of *Sylvia*, thus refers in his Diary to a visit paid on March 16th, 1683:- "I went to see Sir Josiah Child's prodigious cost in planting walnut trees about his seate and making fish ponds many miles in circuit in Epping Forest in, a barren spot, as oftimes these suddainly monied men for the most part seate themselves. He, from a merchant's apprentice, and management of the East India Company's stock, being ariv'd to an estate ('tis said) of £200,000; and lately married his daughter[xcii] to the eldest sonn of the Duke of Beaufort, late Marques of Worcester, with £50,000 portional present, and various expectations." The remains of Sir Josiah Child's tree-planting may still be seen in the beautiful avenue of limes, known as Bush Wood.

Sir Josiah was created a Baronet in 1678, and died in 1699; he was buried in the old church at Wanstead. His monument may still be seen in the chancel of the present church; it is in good preservation, and bears on its front a long inscription in Latin.

SIR JOSIAH CHILD was succeeded at Wanstead by his eldest surviving son, Sir Josiah II[xciii]; he died in 1704 without issue, and was succeeded by his brother, Sir Richard, the third Baronet[xciv]. Sir Richard was created Viscount Castlemaine in 1718, and Earl Tylney of Castlemaine in 1731. In 1715, while still Sir Richard Child, he pulled down the old manor house, and from plans prepared by Colin Campbell[xcv], he built near its site a structure of great magnificence. It is stated that if the original design had been carried out, Wanstead House would have been without a parallel in Europe. An old writer speaks of it as being superior to Blenheim and other

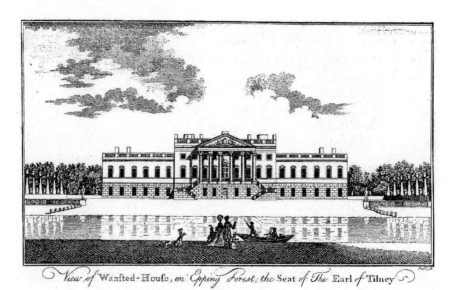

View of Wanfted-Houfe, on Epping Forest; the Seat of The Earl of Tilney

houses. As it was, standing in its own extensive park and surrounded by gardens and pleasure grounds, there were very few houses which rivalled it in England.

It was constructed of Portland stone, and covered an area 260 feet long by seventy feet deep. The main front was adorned in the centre by a noble portico of six Corinthian columns, approached by a double flight of stone steps. In the tympanum were the family arms, finely sculptured, and over the door leading into the great hall was a medallion of the architect. This hall contained a vast variety of ornaments and paintings by the best masters in Italy. The building consisted of two stories, and contained fifty-eight rooms, besides domestic offices. The garden front had no portico, but the pediment was enriched with a bas-relief, and supported by six three-quarter columns. The dining-room, on the left of the hall, was twenty- four feet square, and adjoining it was a drawing-room of the same size. On the right of the hall was another dining-room, twenty-five feet square, and a drawing-room thirty feet by twenty-five feet. On the chimney-piece of one of the drawing-rooms was the representation of an eagle taking up a snake, elegantly cut in white marble, and from this room was an entrance to a bed chamber, from which was a passage into the ballroom, which was seventy feet by twenty-five feet.

Sir Richard Child began laying out the gardens and pleasure grounds before the house was built, spending enormous sums for these purposes. Unfortunately, the gardens were destroyed at the wreckage of the house hereinafter referred to, but Sir Richard's lakes and canals, and the plantations upon their banks still remain[xcvi].

The grotto, referred to later on, is supposed to have been erected by the second Lord Tylney, but I incline to the belief that it was part of Sir Richard's scheme[xcvii].

The chief entrance to the house and park was on the west. It was approached by means of a magnificent avenue of limes, which originally extended from the pond at Leytonstone up to the park gates. This avenue still remains, with others radiating from it, and during the summer months, is greatly patronised by holiday makers and school parties. It does not form part of the land enclosed as Wanstead Park. At the top of the avenue, the road skirted a circular lake[xcviii] in front of the house, extending considerably beyond the extremities of the mansion, which, from this approach, had an aspect of much grandeur. This lake is not in the park, but can be seen from the footpath leading from Blake Hall Road to Wanstead Church.

The first Earl died in March, 1750, and was succeeded by his grandson[xcix], John, as the second Earl. He lived a great many years in Italy, where doubtless he collected many of the art treasures mentioned as being at Wanstead. His continued absence, however, gave rise to much comment, and it was stated by a writer of the period, "that so magnificent a palace should not be left to a handful of servants, and that as Lord Tylney had no heirs, he hoped that ere long the estate would pass into the hands of some other family who would prefer English freedom to Italian slavery." His wishes were soon realised, for a few years afterward, in 1784, the second Lord Tylney died, and the title became extinct. Wanstead then passed to his nephew, Sir James Long, Bart.[c], who took the name of Tylney. Lord Tylney, though he lived so much abroad, appears to have been very proud of his mansion. Horace Walpole[ci] writes of him and the place in a letter to Richard Bentley, on 17th July, 1775:-

> "I dined at Wanstead; many years have passed since I saw it. The disposition of the house and prospect are better than I expected, and very fine. The garden, which they tell me cost as much as the house, that is, £100,000, is wretched; the furniture fine, but without taste. The present Earl is the most generous creature in the world. In the first chamber I entered he offered me four marble tables ; they lay in cases about the room. I compounded (after forty refusals of everything I commended) by bringing away only a haunch of venison. I believe he has not had so cheap a visit a good while. I commend myself, as I ought, for to be sure there were twenty ebony chairs and a couch and a table that would have tried the virtue of a philosopher of double my size."

Sir James Tylney-Long died in 1794, leaving a young son and three daughters. The son having died in infancy, Wanstead became the property of the eldest daughter, Catherine Tylney-Long[cii]. During her minority Wanstead House was appropriated as a residence for the Prince of Condé[ciii], Louis XVIII[civ], and other members of the exiled Bourbon family, for some time previous to the return of peace, in 1814, which restored the King of France, with the Princes of the blood, to the possession of the throne of his ancestors.

Miss Catherine Tylney-Long was now one of the richest heiresses in England; for her estate was valued at £80,000 a year. She had many suitors, and it is said even royalty tried its best to secure her hand in marriage. The prize was eventually won by the Hon. William Pole-Wellesley[cv], only son of Lord Maryborough, afterwards Earl of Mornington. They were married on March 14th, 1812, with great ceremony at St. James's Church, Piccadilly, when the bridegroom assumed the additional names of Tylney and Long, and blossomed out with the surname of Pole-Tylney-Long- Wellesley. Under this name he figured in a celebrated book of the period, Smith's *REJECTED ADDRESSES*, in the single line:- "Long may Long-Tilney-Wellesley-Long-Pole live."

The following details of the dress of the bride and bride-groom are taken from the newspapers of the time. The dress of the bride was a robe of real Brussels point lace placed over white satin, her bonnet was of Brussels lace ornamented with two ostrich feathers. She also wore a deep lace veil and a white satin pelisse, trimmed with swansdown. The dress cost 700 guineas, the bonnet 150 guineas, and the veil 200 guineas. Mr. Pole-Wellesley wore a plain blue coat with yellow buttons, a white waistcoat, buff breeches and white silk stockings. The lady's jewels consisted principally of a brilliant necklace and earrings, the former costing 20,000 guineas. Every domestic in the family of Lady Tylney-Long, the bride's mother, was liberally provided for.

The following description of a party at Wanstead is from The Globe newspaper of August 3rd, 1812:-

*On Friday last, Mr. and Mrs. Tylney Long Wellesley gave a
magnificent entertainment at their princely chateau at Wanstead, in*

Essex. It was introduced as a complimentary tribute to the Duke of Cambridge[cvi], and the several officers who Inspected the three regiments of East India Volunteers in the spacious plain in Tylney Park. It was a banquet of the most sumptuous description, and took place about four o'clock in the afternoon, immediately sub- sequent to the review. Forty persons sat down to dinner in the great saloon. The company comprehended all the particular friends of the family, including Lady Catherine and her daughter, Mrs. and Miss Wellesley Pole (the near relations of the ex-Secretary in Ireland), Lady Smith Burgess[cvii], &c.

Young, rich, the bride of a future peer, and the possessor of a necklace worth 20,000 guineas-surely the lot of Wanstead's lady was cast in pleasant places, and she had a goodly heritage. But the conclusion of the story is one that may make us inclined to weep. It would have been better for this unhappy lady had she married "for love" the poorest labourer on her estate.

Mr. Wellesley was about as perfect a specimen of the genus scamp as could well be imagined. Deeply in debt at the time, it is clear that he married Miss Tylney-Long solely for her property, and having got it safely in his fingers he next proceeded to squander it. At the present time we hear occasionally of fortunes wasted, but even to us it seems incredible that this spendthrift could get through his wife's magnificent fortune in the small space of ten years[cviii].

In June, 1822, his broken-hearted wife had to see the furniture and contents of the house in which her early days were spent[cix], swept away under the auctioneer's hammer to pay her husband's debts. The sale of the wonderful collection of furniture and art treasures which her ancestors had collected at such an outlay of money, time and care, naturally occasioned great excitement. The auctioneer was the celebrated George Robins[cx]; the sale commenced on June 13th, 1822, and lasted for thirty-two days. The amount realised was £41,000. Among the objects of antiquarian interest disposed of were the celebrated ebony chairs and sofa, which have been already mentioned in the extract from Horace Walpole's letter for their

singular beauty and antique character. They were purchased by Graham, of Waterloo Place, by whom they were sold to Lord MacDonald.

In the public Free Library, at Stratford, is a copy of the catalogue of the sale of the furniture which contains 401 pages. This copy is marked at places with the prices realised.

The sale of the furniture was a mere stop-gap. The portraits of his wife's family had not been put up at this time, but even these subsequently shared the same fate, being sold in 1851, at the auction rooms of Messrs. Christie and Manson.

At the time of the sale of the furniture, Wanstead House was also offered, but as no purchaser could be found, the magnificent mansion was pulled down in the following year and the material sold piecemeal in separate lots, so that the creditors might get what they could by carrying away its stones. A writer of the day thus graphically refers to this: -

> "In the latter part of the XVIII century, Wanstead House still displayed all the splendour which the Childs, the Tylneys, and the Longs have lavished upon a palace fit for the abode of gentle and royal blood. Little did I dream that in one quarter of a century I should see its proud columns prostrated in the dust, its decorations annihilated, its pictures and sculptures dispersed by the magic of the hammer. At one period simply a deserted mansion, at another a refuge for exiled princes, then for a brief space polluted by riot and profligacy, and ultimately its lawns and gardens swept away, its stately groves and avenues remorselessly destroyed, and myself present at the sad catastrophe. Such, however, were its short and painful annals, and, except the grotto, not one stone remains upon another. A palace destined to stand for ages, and upon which time had made no inroads, was removed by permission of the Lord Chancellor, when little more than a hundred winters had passed over it, when its features were just mellowed, its woods and plantations in full luxuriance, and all around it smiling in perfection."

Wanstead House was the most attractive of its kind near London, and a national ornament. The writer goes on to lament that the government had not purchased it for some national institution, scientific or educational, sarcastically adding his belief that:-

> "It would not have been allowed to perish if the walls had been covered with ivy and the fabric been in the last state of decay. "I was familiar with every bower and secluded avenue, I knew where its blossoms were fairest and its fruit choicest, could thread the mazes of its delightful foliage and exotic gardens, its limpid waters and its verdant lawns, all which I have visited at dawn, at sunset, at mid-day, and at night.

> "A turf-covered mound is all that remains to mark the spot of Wanstead House. A few yards west of this mound, a spacious lake, which formerly mirrored the front of the magnificent building, still lies

bosomed in the hill-top, while further on beyond the remains of the grand entrance-gates, some portion of the avenues, which, in former times, radiated in several directions may yet be seen. Northward stands the church, and almost hidden by a clump of trees some farm buildings still remain to bear it company. Southward, at the foot of the slope, lie spread out numerous lakes and pools."

Hunting the red deer in Epping Forest was one of the amusements of the "Dis-Honourable."

A writer in Bailey's Magazine some years ago said:-

"The limits of the grand old forest have been grievously curtailed since the days when Mr. Long-Pole-Wellesley played high jinks at Wanstead House, where he kept a pack of stag-hounds in a style of princely magnificence to hunt the wild deer. His servants were dressed in Lincoln green. There were constant hunt breakfasts at the "Eagle," at Snaresbrook, then in the middle of an open waste, where all were entertained at Mr. Wellesley's expense. Everything was done with the most reckless extravagance, and he would scatter sovereigns to countrymen in the hunting field as readily as other liberal sportsmen would give shillings or sixpences."

It seems strange to this generation to hear of wild deer hunting within nine miles of the stones of London streets. Eventually, as many of these wild deer as could be caught were taken to Windsor Park, but a few remained and served as sport to local huntsmen, until the last old stag, after a great run, was killed at West Ham.

On the sale of the house, the "Dis-Honourable" did not wait to see what became of his paupered wife and children. Pursued by his creditors, he escaped down the river Thames in an open boat. Need we wonder that in three years after the spoliation of her home we read of the death of the unhappy lady through a broken heart? She left two children[cxi]. Surely, it was a happy release. Few histories can equal in sadness that of the House of Wanstead and this story of the brokenhearted Catherine Tylney-Long. It

INTERIOR OF GROTTO BEFORE THE FIRE, from a Photo. by Mr. G. W. DUNN, of Woodford

would be almost impossible to find another case in which a life with such bright prospects came to so sudden and premature an end.

But, although the "Dis-Honourable" has sold the furniture that his wife brought him, the portraits of her ancestors, and the very stones that covered her head in infancy, and has, as a matter of fact, passed out of my sphere as the historian of Wanstead, I cannot resist following him in his later days. On the death of his uncle, in 1842, and the consequent accession of his father to the Earldom of Mornington, he became Viscount Wellesley, and three years later, on the death of his father, he succeeded to the title of Earl of Mornington. He had not long remained a widower, for in 1828, probably with the object of retrieving his shattered fortunes, he married as his second wife[cxii], the daughter of Colonel Thomas Paterson. How he treated this lady may be gathered from the following extract from the Athenæum, in referring to her death in 1869:-

"The Countess of Mornington, widow of the 'notorious' William-Pole-Tylney-Long- Wellesley, Earl of Mornington, who died recently, in her seventy-sixth year, adds an incident to the romance of the peerage. In the ruin in which the reckless Earl fell some forty years ago (that is to say only about twelve months after her marriage), this lady was for a brief time an inmate of St. George's Workhouse, and more than once had to apply at Police Courts for temporary relief."

He died in 1857, and was succeeded by his son, who died unmarried in 1863. On his death, the Earldom of Mornington and other titles passed to his cousin, the second Duke of Wellington[cxiii]. But before the "Dis-Honourable's" death, he was for years a pensioner of the great Duke.

Again, it will be noticed how curiously history is interwoven with Wanstead. The flight of the French King to England, and his subsequent stay at Wanstead was, of course, due to Napoleon Bonaparte. It is singular that upon a member of the Wellesley family, the Duke of Wellington, should fall the destiny of effecting the downfall of Napoleon. In the light of subsequent events, one little incident of the "Dis-Honourable's" occupancy of Wanstead may be recorded. Twelve months after his marriage to Miss Tylney-Long, he did on one occasion come before the public with regard to the estate which his wife had brought him. It was an attempt to shut up a public way through the park, but at the trial at Chelmsford Assizes, he utterly failed to secure his end[cxiv]. If his ghost ever visits Wanstead Park, it will be interested in the fact that every inch of the place is now the property of the people.

AS already stated, the manor of Wanstead, with adjacent land became the property of another Wellesley, and eventually of Lord Cowley[cxv].

THE WATER GATE—GROTTO.

Nothing now remains of the house; some farm buildings[cxvi] are still to be seen at the rear of Wanstead Church and a building called "the Temple[cxvii]," which stands to the east of the Refreshment Chalet[cxviii], and the Grotto. The garden has been ploughed into grazing land.

At this stage the Corporation of London purchased the ornamental portion of the estate, now known as Wanstead Park (comprising the woods, waters, and heronry, made by Sir Richard Child), and conveyed it to the Epping Forest Committee in trust for the people.

The portion purchased contained about 184 acres. It was effected by an exchange of fifty acres (of great value for building purposes, but of little or no value to the public) and the payment of £8,000 as a makeweight to Lord Cowley, the latter agreeing to fence off the park from his other land and to make a road a mile long to give access to the park at either end, to Forest Gate at one end and Snaresbrook at the other.

The park is practically, therefore, an addition to Epping Forest, but the grounds round the great lakes are closed at night.

Wanstead Park was formally opened to the public by the Epping Forest Committee on August 1st, 1882.

The *City Press*, in the report of the proceedings, says:- "It may not inappropriately be termed the finishing touch to the work of the Corporation in the east of London."

Mr. Deputy Hora, the chairman of the Epping Forest Committee, in the absence of the Duke of Connaught[cxix] (the Chief Ranger), performed the ceremony of declaring the park open. He said that "Her Majesty the Queen[cxx] had opened Epping Forest to the people on May 6th, and that they (the Committee) were present that day to open the beautiful grounds of Wanstead Park, also for the public use for ever, thus completing the work which the Corporation had been engaged in for some years, and by which a stop was put to the encroachment which had been going on. Wanstead Park consisted of about 184 acres, of which thirty acres were ornamental water."

In securing this park on the southern side of Epping Forest, the Corporation made a great acquisition in favour of the public. This beautiful piece of woodland and water was necessary to relieve the flatness of this portion of the county, and place the people living in the south on equal terms with those who lived in the north portion of the forest.

The park is maintained in its wild and rustic appearance. No attempt has been made to cut or trim it into a garden, except the necessary clearance of such underwood as would tend to destroy the growth of the trees.

The uniform dress of the keepers is that pertaining to the forest, and not to the park.

The Grotto.

The remains of the grotto will be found near the lakes. At the time of pulling down the house in 1822, this erection was apparently overlooked. It was a beautiful structure in a style which was fashionable in the last century. A chamber with a domed roof was encrusted with pebbles, shells, stalactites, crystals, and looking glasses; and a fine painted window added at great expense by the Countess of Mornington The tessellated pavement is made of the small bones of deer. It is stated to have cost not less than £40,000, but it is to be hoped that this is an exaggeration. In the Beauties of England it is stated that the cost of the structure of this grotto was £2,000, independent of its costly material. It was considered finer than the grotto[cxxi] connected with Pope's Villa at Twickenham, so often referred to in books of history and poetry. It was burnt down in November, 1884.

Situated upon the border of the lakes, the view from its windows must have been enchanting. An old map shows that the river Roding formerly flowed through this lake, which was then at a lower level. At a subsequent date the course of the river, which now bounds the park on that side, was cut to enable the level of the lake to be raised, an operation which had the effect of widening the channels and partly submerging a curious structure called "The Fortification."

From a plan dated 1735, in the possession of the trustees for the Earl of Mornington, and prepared by a French landscape gardener named Roche[cxxii], who seems to have had the idea of converting Wanstead into another Versailles, it appears that several other rectangular sheets of water were projected, which were not carried out.

The Heronry.

One of the most interesting features of the park is the herony. The birds originally made their home on the island in the Heronry Pond, from which fact the pond derives its name, but many years ago they migrated to the Lincoln Island, where they have ever since built their nests at the top of the highest trees. In moving from the old home to the new, the herons unquestionably exercised an instinct which is strongly akin to reason, for there cannot be two

THE HOME OF THE HERONS.

opinions as to which is the most desirable place of abode. These birds usually come to the heronry about the beginning of February, and at once begin patching up their old nests, or building fresh ones. Although a few remain through the winter, the greater number leave the heronry towards the middle of the summer. The admission of the public to the park does not seem to have interfered with their breeding.

The Heronry Lake was reconstructed and enlarged during the winter of 1906-7. The work was done by the unemployed, under the direction of the West Ham Distress Committee. The cost was £10,400, and 2,022 men

47

altogether were employed for various periods. The enlarged lake now covers an area of 12¾ acres, with an average depth of from 3ft. 6in. to 4ft; the water is supplied from the Shoulder of Mutton Pond. One of the islands was much increased in size, and a new one was made, called Buxton Island. The opening ceremony was performed on July 6th, 1907, by Alderman and Mrs. Spratt, the Mayor and Mayoress of West Ham. Mrs. Spratt was presented with a number of flint arrow-heads which were found during the excavation.

Although the park is diversified with grassland and wood, coppice and lawn, the lakes[cxxiii] form its chief attraction. Upon some, boating, fishing, or bathing is permited. Others are preserved as much as possible in the natural state to which time brought them during the period from 1822 to 1882. It is impossible to describe in words the charm of the lakes, or even to portray their beauties by photography. To sit near the Grotto as the dusk falls on a summer evening is an experience which can never be forgotten. Instead of attempting to portray it, I urge my readers to visit the spot and enjoy it for themselves.

It is somewhat unfortunate that in the purchase a little more could not have been done as to the matter of entrance. Thus from the Snaresbrook side, it would appear that a very easy and natural entrance could have been made by continuing the road leading to Wanstead Church, which ends abruptly at the church gates; and presuming this had been done, the old park gates could have been utilised for the visitors coming from the north portion of Leytonstone by the footpath. Indeed, one wonders why the pond in front of Wanstead Church, the one which was before the old house, was not taken into the park grounds. A convenient entrance, however, has been opened in the Blake Hall Road, which serves for the Leytonstone folk, opposite the Evelyn Avenue, and visitors from Forest Gate can either use this or the one in the bridle road from Wanstead to Ilford, near Lake's Farm. From Ilford and and Manor Park the easiest entrance is across Wanstead Flats.

Roman Antiquities.

On the south side of the lower part of the gardens of Wanstead, nearly adjoining Aldersbrook, a tessellated pavement was discovered in 1715, by

48

some labourers, when digging holes to plant an avenue of trees from the gardens. The owner would not at the time permit it to be laid quite bare. Its extent from north to south was about twenty feet, and from east to west about sixteen feet. It consisted of small squares of brick and marble of divers colours, and from an inch to an inch and a quarter square. The outside was a border about a foot broad, composed of red tesserae about three-quarters of an inch square, within which were several ornaments, and in the centre a figure of a man mounted on some beast and holding something in his right hand. This pavement was situated on a gentle gravel ascent towards the north, and at a small distance from the south end of it was a spring or well of fine water, now absorbed in one of the great lakes. From this well the ground rose gradually towards the south till it came to an exact level, which reaches a long way. On the very brink of this level, and about three hundred yards directly south from the before- mentioned well and pavement, were the remains of some brick foundations; and some years after, upon making further improvements, the workmen found broken pots and fragments of urns of different kinds of earth, some brown, some white, but all of coarse clay, and many pieces of brick, which proved there had been a building there, and many calcined human bones, teeth, etc. A small copper coin of the Emperor Valens[cxxiv], a silver medal and another copper coin estimated to be of the Constantine age[cxxv], were likewise found here. Mr. Smart Lethieullier[cxxvi] considered the pavement to have been that of a banqueting room belonging to a Roman villa and that the place where the urns and bones were found was probably the mausoleum of some private family, whose villa stood on more elevated ground, probably where Wanstead House stood. The presence of the urns signified that the bodies were burnt, for although burning was abolished by the Romans and burying adopted, it took some time for Christianity to become established, and for the act of burial to become general.

EVELYN AVENUE IN BUSH WOOD, WANSTEAD FLATS.

How the Park was purchased for the People[cxxvii].

It should never be forgotten that it was due to the stupendous efforts of the Corporation of London, brought about mainly by the untiring labours of Mr. John T. Bedford[cxxviii], that Wanstead Park and Epping Forest was secured to the people.

It will not be out of place to record this memorable struggle, and the way in which the Corporation were able to find money for the purchase of the Forest and Wanstead Park.

In ancient times the Corporation possessed the right to measure and tax all corn that entered the port of London. Modern innovations in the corn trade made this regulation very irksome; so, after consultation with the members of the corn trade, the Corporation consented to give up its right, which produced about £9,000 a year, if Parliament would grant it a small tax for a limited period upon foreign corn entering the port, the proceeds of which

50

they undertook to devote to the preservation of open spaces. This was accordingly done, and in 1872 an Act was passed, and under its provisions the Corporation was empowered for thirty years to levy a tax of three-quarters of a farthing upon every hundredweight of corn entering the port of London.

Taxes are considered obnoxious things, as a rule, and this one was described as "a grievous burden upon the food of the poor," but as it is necessary to eat seventy-five half- quartern loaves before the tax amounts to one farthing, it is not one that many people could object to. And as it chanced that most of our corn at the time of the purchase of Epping Forest and Wan-stead came from America, it may fairly be stated that the American farmers bought Epping Forest and Wanstead Park for us, an act of generosity on their part which we appreciate none the less because they probably knew nothing about it. Such is the enormous trade in foreign corn, however, that this insignificant tax brings in over £40,000 a year.

Now, the lords of the manors about Epping Forest had certain ancient rights of pasturage and pannage in the Forest. Not satisfied with this, they shamefully encroached upon the forest land, putting up fences around such pieces adjacent to their own property as seemed to them desirable to make such property the more valuable. The Governments of those days were criminally careless in looking after the public rights. Between the years 1854 and 1863 they had grossly sold the Crown rights in the Forest for some £18,000 (less than £5 per acre), and where the money went to has never been found out to this day. In 1850 the Forest comprised almost 6,000 acres. During the ensuring twenty years, half this area was surrounded by fences and partly built upon.

It was in 1871 that the battle for the people began. Public opinion had been excited considerably by the barefaced robberies. A right reverend Bishop had, for instance, enclosed one little acre. A reverend gentleman, the shepherd of a neighbouring flock, had completely enclosed one thousand acres-worth to him, if he could only have stuck to it, about £180,000. It is interesting to know that, having completed his little job, on the following Sunday he preached to his amused congregation (who knew all about it) from the text, "The love of money is the root of all evil." A noble and right honourable Earl appropriated five hundred and seventy acres, and when called to account, indignantly denied it, and stated through his agent that he had only five hundred and sixty-three acres. A gallant admiral had not only enclosed a goodly portion of the Forest, but had announced his intention of cutting down the timber on it. The Court of Chancery, however, soon showed him that, though he could "shiver his timbers," he could not shiver the timbers of the people.

It is all very well for a public body to sympathise with a movement, but it cannot always show its sympathy in a practical way. The Corporation, probably through some of its members living in the neighbourhood, knew of the growing agitation. Cogitations followed, and by a bit of luck the Corporation found itself in position to take up and fight the battle of the people.

On the east side of Wanstead lies the City of London Cemetery[cxxix]. It is remarkable that this last resting place of the dead became the stepping-stone to the restoration of Epping Forest to the living; for, if the land for this cemetery had not been acquired by the Corporation (the City Commission of Sewers), it would not have been in the position legally to maintain the right to break down the encroachments of the land-grabbers.

The land upon which the cemetery was made was the ancient Manor of Aldersbrook, and in the time of James I the lord of this manor claimed for himself and his tenants the right of common and pasture for their beasts, throughout the length and breadth of the forest wastes.

Upon this the Corporation, when it had resolved to help the public, based its claim to interfere, and so the City authorities gave instructions for the preparation of a Bill in Chancery to dispossess these pirates of the land they had stolen.

During the Chancery proceedings, injunctions were obtained against the various defendants to prevent further damage. One of these was the gallant admiral already mentioned. Another was a man, caught red-handed, so to speak, who, plough in hand, was breaking up what is called Bush Wood, at Wanstead, where the great avenues are a most glorious spot. Although he

stated he was only breaking up an odd corner, it was found he had taken a lease of the whole place at 30s. an acre, on the condition that he broke it all up.

It was not until 1874 that the chancery suit was ready to be tried. It had taken three years to prepare the case. There were seventeen defendants. It was tried before the Master of the Rolls, Sir George Jessel, and occupied twenty-three days in the hearing. It was a serious moment for the Corporation when the Judge commenced his judgment, for if the day was lost, the costs would amount to £100,000.

But the matter was not long left in doubt. Sir George Jessel's decision was clear and emphatic. "These persons [the defendants] have taken what did not belong to them, without the consent of the owners, and have applied it to their own purpose, and have endeavoured to support their title by a large amount of false evidence." It was fortunate for the worthy bishop, reverend minister, noble earl and gallant admiral that these words had not been

53

uttered at the Old Bailey, for if they had, picking oakum, with the treadmill as a physical recreation, might have been their reward.

No attempt was ever made to upset Sir George Jessel's[cxxx] judgment. Important as the decision was, it was not all, for it left matters at a curious point. For it was stated during the trial that even if the Corporation gained the day it would stop encroachment by the lords of the manors, but it would not enable the public to have access to and enjoy the forest. The law as to common land was stated by Sir William Harcourt[cxxxi] (who was one of the counsel in the case) to be this: " No one has a legal right to go on a common, but if he chooses to go on no one has a legal right to turn him off." I have put in this singularly beautiful bit of old English law so that it shall not be lost to coming generations.

The Corporation, flushed with victory, determined that no doubt should remain as to Epping Forest. As soon as the case was settled, steps were taken to buy up the rights of the lords of the manors, costing £110,000, and the Corporation therefore became the owner of the land, as trustees for the people. The ultimate result was, that about 5,530 acres were secured to the public. The entire cost to the Corporation was about £247,000.

Wanstead Church[cxxxii].

Wanstead Church, dedicated to the Virgin Mary, was repaired and enlarged in the early part of the last century, principally at the expense of the first Lord Tylney; but, being still found small and incommodious, it was resolved, at the instance of Dr. Glasse[cxxxiii], the then Rector, to pull it down and build a new church on a larger scale, nearly adjoining the old site. This church was finished in 1790. The expense of building the Church was £9,000. The subscriptions received amounted to £3,000, the remainder being raised by a tontine. The building is of brick, cased with Portland stone, and having a portico of the Doric order. At the west end is a cupola, supported by eight Ionic columns. The inside is extremely neat and elegant. It consists of chancel, nave, and two aisles, supported by columns of the Corinthian order.

The pavement, which is remarkable for its beauty, is of stone brought from Painswick, in Gloucestershire. In the chancel is a beautiful window of stained glass, representing our Saviour bearing the Cross, from the picture at Magdalen College. In the east window of the north aisle are the royal arms; in the south, the arms of the late Sir John Tylney-Long, Bart. In the chancel is a superb monument in white marble, to the memory of Sir Josiah Child, Bart., who died in 1699; it was removed from the old church, and consists of a recumbent life-size figure.

In the churchyard was buried, in 1647, John Saltmarsh[cxxxiv], a noted Puritan and divine.

Wanstead is rich in memories of celebrated persons. Dr. Pound[cxxxv], Rector from 1707 to 1724, was a great scientist, especially in astronomy, and a personal friend of Sir Isaac Newton[cxxxvi], who visited him there. Sir Isaac Newton was the founder of the house of opticians of that name, and his descendants still carry on business in Fleet Street, close to the Strand. When the maypole[cxxxvii], which once flourished in the Strand, was taken out in 1717, it was purchased by Sir Isaac, and presented to Dr. Pound, who had it erected in Wanstead Park, and used it as a support for his telescope, which at that time was the largest known-125 feet long. Still greater even than Dr. Pound was his nephew, James Bradley[cxxxviii], who after-wards became Astronomer Royal. He studied a method of calculating the velocity of light.

Lake House.

At a short distance to the south-west of the site of Wanstead House stood a building called Lake House[cxxxix]. This was built to be an appendage to Wanstead House, and was originally a banqueting hall or summer house. In it for many years Tom Hood[cxl] resided. The house was more generally known as the Russian farm. In a description of this building by Thomas Hood, jun., in a memoir of his father, the author writes: "The fact was, it had been formerly a sort of banqueting hall to Wanstead Park, and the rest of the house was sacrificed to one great room, which extended all along the back. There was a beautiful chimney-piece carved in fruit and flowers, by Grinling Gibbons[cxli], and the ceiling bore traces of painting. Several quaint

Watteau-like[cxlii] pictures of the seasons were panelled on the walls, but it was all in a shocking state of repair. In the twilight the rats used to come and peep out of the holes in the wainscot. There were two or three windows, whilst a door in the middle opened on to a flight of steps leading into a pleasant wilderness of a garden, infested by hundreds of rabbits from the warren close by. From the windows one could catch lovely glimpses of forest scenery, especially one fine aspen avenue. In the midst of the garden lay a little lake, from which the house took its name, surrounded by high masses of rhododendrons. It was in this house that Hood wrote the novel, *Tilney Hall*, much of the descriptive scenery being taken from Wanstead and its neighbourhood, and here he also wrote a little volume containing a poem, entitled *The Epping Hunt*."

Wanstead Flats.

This expanse of four hundred acres, formerly a very favourite place for the gipsy tribe, lies southward of Wanstead Park, and is fringed on its south side by Forest Gate and Manor Park. It was secured by the Government for military operations. George III[cxliii] held a review of 10,000 troops on the flats in the early part of the last century, and military displays continued down to 1874.

During recent periods of depression in trade, a good deal of labour has been spent upon the flats in draining and making suitable grounds for cricket and tennis. Excellent as such an idea may be, it should not be permitted to go too far.

This magnificent stretch of flat land is remarkable for the purity and freshness of its air, and the privilege to roam at will over it is more valuable than that a few places should be reserved for cricket, etc. It is a curious fact that a straight line from Wanstead Flats to a point easterly of the North Pole would not pass any town or large village in England, nor would any other inhabited country be touched. When the wind is in this quarter, it comes to Wanstead singularly crisp and clean.

West Ham Park[cxliv].

In addition to Epping Forest and Wanstead Park, the Corporation also contributed to West Ham Park £17,000 out of the fund available for open spaces. The cost of maintenance of these parks is, however, paid for out of its private purse. The management of West Ham Park is also vested in the Epping Forest Committee, and the Wanstead Flats and Wanstead Park may be said to form the starting point of Epping Forest.

REPLIES

Sir Henry Mildmay (Vol. IX, p. 276).

-The October instalment of Mr. Dawson's valuable article on Wanstead begins by stating that Sir Henry Mildmay was the purchaser of Wanstead, and lower down suggests that it was given to him by King James. I have it that he bought it with his wife's money from the Duke of Buckingham, and that it was said to be worth £1000 per annum at that time. It is also stated that Sir Henry sat three times at the trial of Charles I, but in fact he sat on January 6th, 10th, 15th, 20th, 23rd (twice), 25th and 26th-eight times out of the twenty-two sittings; once in Westminster Hall, and the other times in the Painted Chamber. Alderman Haliday's name is spelt with one l on his tomb in St. Lawrence Jewry Church.

-Herbert St. John-Mildmay, Lieut-Col.

THE REFRESHMENT CHALET.

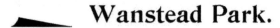

THE CHÂLET, ⸗

Wanstead Park.

Parties and School Treats catered for on reasonable terms.

58

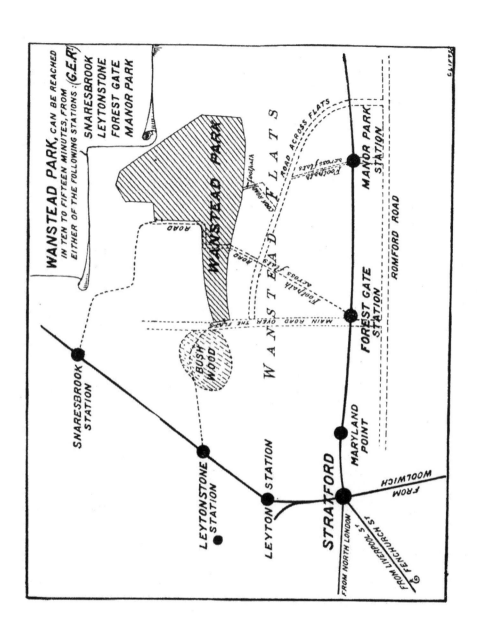

WANSTEAD PARK, CAN BE REACHED IN TEN TO FIFTEEN MINUTES, FROM EITHER OF THE FOLLOWING STATIONS : (G.E.Rʸ)
SNARESBROOK
LEYTONSTONE
FOREST GATE
MANOR PARK

WANSTEAD PARK

WANSTEAD FLATS

BUSH WOOD

ROAD

Footpath across flats

Footpath across flats

Footpath across the Flats

MAIN ROAD OVER THE FLATS

ROAD ACROSS FLATS

ROMFORD ROAD

MANOR PARK STATION

FOREST GATE STATION

SNARESBROOK STATION

LEYTONSTONE STATION

LEYTON STATION

MARYLAND POINT

STRATFORD

FROM WOOLWICH

FROM NORTH LONDON

FROM LIVERPOOL Sᵗ

FENCHURCH Sᵗ

GREAT EASTERN RAILWAY. Wanstead Park.

Trains leave LIVERPOOL STREET, FENCHURCH STREET, and intermediate Stations at frequent intervals throughout the day, for FOREST GATE, MANOR PARK, ILFORD, LEYTONSTONE, and SNARESBROOK Stations.

RETURN TICKETS ARE ISSUED AS UNDER:

To	From Liverpool Street.			From Fenchurch Street.		
	1st Class	2nd Class	3rd Class	1st Class	2nd Class	3rd Class
	s. d.	s. d.	s. d.	s. d.	s. d.	s. d.
FOREST GATE	1 1	0 10	0 7	1 0	0 9	0 6
MANOR PARK	1 4	1 1	0 9	1 0	0 9	0 7
ILFORD	1 7	1 1	0 10	1 5	1 0	0 9
LEYTONSTONE	1 4	1 1	0 9	1 3	1 0	0 8
SNARESBROOK	1 7	1 4	0 11	1 6	1 3	0 10

These tickets are available for return on the same or following day; those issued on Saturday are available to return up to the Monday following.

CHEAP EXCURSIONS IN ESSEX.
BILLERICAY, BURNHAM-ON-CROUCH, and SOUTHMINSTER.

ON THURSDAYS and SATURDAYS during the Summer months CHEAP HALF-DAY RETURN EXCURSION TICKETS are issued at STRATFORD MARKET, MARYLAND POINT, FOREST GATE, MANOR PARK, and ILFORD STATIONS, as under:—

To BILLERICAY .... 1st Class 2/-, 3rd Class 1/-

To BURNHAM-ON-CROUCH } " 3/-, " 1/6.
and SOUTHMINSTER .... }

For Particulars of Trains and other Excursion Arrangements, see small bills, to be obtained at the Stations.

Liverpool Street Station, *August*, 1894.

WILLIAM BIRT, *General Manager.*

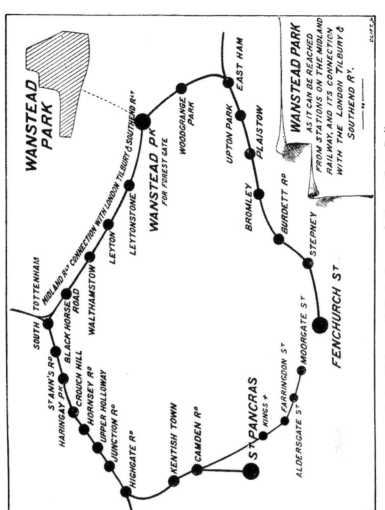

WANSTEAD PARK

WANSTEAD PK
FOR FOREST GATE

WANSTEAD PARK
AS IT CAN BE REACHED
FROM STATIONS ON THE MIDLAND
RAILWAY, AND ITS CONNECTION
WITH THE LONDON TILBURY &
SOUTHEND RY.

EAST HAM
UPTON PARK
PLAISTOW
BROMLEY
BURDETT RD
STEPNEY
FENCHURCH ST

WOODGRANGE PARK
MIDLAND RLY CONNECTION WITH LONDON TILBURY & SOUTHEND RLY
LEYTONSTONE
LEYTON
WALTHAMSTOW
BLACK HORSE ROAD
SOUTH TOTTENHAM
ST ANN'S RD
HARINGAY PK
CROUCH HILL
HORNSEY RD
UPPER HOLLOWAY
JUNCTION RD
HIGHGATE RD
KENTISH TOWN
CAMDEN RD
ST PANCRAS
KINGS +
FARRINGDON ST
ALDERSGATE ST
MOORGATE ST

Ask for Tickets *viâ* Tottenham and Forest Gate Railway.

MIDLAND and LONDON, TILBURY and SOUTHEND RAILWAYS

(via Tottenham and Forest Gate Railway).

The New Tottenham and Forest Gate Railway

IS NOW OPEN FOR PASSENGER TRAFFIC.

Trains are run at convenient intervals to and from

FENCHURCH STREET (*via* East Ham).
ST. PANCRAS
KING'S CROSS (Metropolitan) } (*via* South Tottenham and Kentish Town).
MOORGATE STREET

Express Trains also run to and from SOUTHEND=ON=SEA by the New and Shorter Route.

CHEAP WEEK-END TICKETS evey Friday and Saturday from St. Pancras, South Tottenham, and intermediate stations to:—

SOUTHEND-ON-SEA, 6/- First Class, 3/6 Third Class. SHOEBURYNESS, 6/8 First Class, 3/10 Third Class. Also **CHEAP DAILY EXCURSIONS** to **SOUTHEND-ON-SEA, 5/- First Class, 2/6 Third Class.**

→ **SPECIAL CHEAP RATES ARE QUOTED FOR PARTIES OF TWENTY OR MORE.** ←

Particulars of the Train Service, Fares, etc., may be had at the Midland and Joint Line Stations, or on application to Mr. Elliott, St. Pancras.

July, 1894.

By ORDER.

62

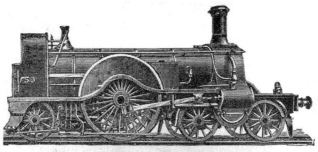

WHY MAKE SMALL TOY-SHOP MODELS

when for same time and trouble you can easily make a valuable and powerful model from our high-class castings and materials. The illustration shows our superb **1 in. scale model, Great Northern Railway Express Locomotive,** 2 ft. 6 in. long, 8 in. driving wheels, cylinders 1½ in. bore, complete set, over 86 castings, in very best soft iron and gun metal, with phototypes to work from, £3 ; usual price £7.

The Editor of *Work* says (28th Jan., 1893)—" Messrs. MARTIN & Co.'s castings for Locomotives (over 80 pieces) are all that could be desired."

The Editor of *The Bazaar* says (3rd June, 1892)—" We have received sundry castings from Mr. W. MARTIN, and are glad to be able to report favourably of them."

Half H.P. Horizontal Engine, finished as illustrated, £10, or a complete set of castings for making this engine, 25/-.

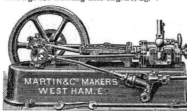

"I have gained a first-class certificate for horizontal engine at Stratford Industrial Exhibition, which I made from a set of your castings."—J. TAFFS, Plaistow.

"The castings give me the greatest satisfaction, also the ½ H.P. vertical boiler."—H. B., Upton Park.

"Splendid metal, design is good."—W. P., Folkestone.

"Have never seen iron castings anything like so good and sound ; shall recommend you."—J. A., Alcester.

3½ in. **Centre Back=Geared Foot Lathe,** with compound slide rest, chucks, and tools, on massive cast-iron standards, with heavy turned driving wheel, improved treadle motion, £15. Castings for making this lathe can be had either rough or machined.

This lathe is designed specially for making high-class model or other machinery.

"The lathe to hand. It gives every satisfaction ; I consider it a beautiful machine."—F. C. S. D., Bournemouth.

"I have received the 3½ in. lathe. Have thoroughly examined it, and am pleased to find it as described—a genuine tool. I shall recommend you to my friends."—H. B., London.

··o◊o··

Originals of testimonials with many others, can be seen at our works.

··o◊o··

W. MARTIN & CO., ENGINEERS AND FOUNDERS,
Albion Works,
EAST ROAD, WEST HAM, ESSEX.

64

MELLIN'S
For Infants FOOD, and Invalids.

THEATRE ROYAL, ROTHERHAM, *May 5th, 1894.*

Dear Sir,—I enclose you a photo. of my two babies, Master George and Miss Jessie Manning (twins), eight months old. As they have been fed upon Mellins Food, I thought perhaps it might interest you.   Yours truly, W. MANNING.

MELLIN'S FOOD BISCUITS
DIGESTIVE. NOURISHING. SUSTAINING.
For Children after Weaning, the Aged, Dyspeptic, and for all who require a simple, nutritious and sustaining Food.

Price 2s. per Tin.

An Illustrated Pamphlet on the Feeding and Rearing of Infants; a Practical and Simple Treatise for Mothers. Containing a large number of Portraits of Healthy and Beautiful Children, together with Facsimiles of Original Testimonials, which are of the greatest interest to all mothers, to be had, with samples, free by post, on application to

MELLIN'S FOOD WORKS, STAFFORD STREET, PECKHAM, S.E.

65

ENDNOTES

[i] The name Epping Forest was first recorded in the seventeenth century. Prior to this it was known as Waltham Forest, and for official purposes long continued to be called this. In terms of its area, the present forest is a mere fragment of its mediaeval predecessor. However, its character is also quite different: prior to the mid-nineteenth century, most of the area of the forest was managed as wood pasture - there were only a few islands of mature woodland. See Milne's land-use maps from c.1800.

[ii] Snaresbrook is a corruption of "Sayes Brook" or "Sayers Brook", the name of a stream which formerly ran through the area.

[iii] "The George" public house (formerly "The George and Dragon"), still a landmark at the south end of Wanstead High Street, is recorded from 1716, but was rebuilt in its present form around 1902. The older building was used for meetings of the Vestry and other local bodies.

[iv] Local Boards existed in urban areas of England and Wales from 1848 to 1894. They had powers to control sewers, clean the streets, regulate slaughterhouses and ensure the proper supply of water to their districts. Local boards were eventually merged with the corporations of municipal boroughs in 1873, or became urban districts in 1894.

[v] A variety of suggestions have been made concerning the derivation of the name Wanstead. It seems clear that 'stead' comes from the Old English "stede" meaning "place" or "house of". However, "wan" could be derived from "wan" meaning white; "wen" meaning a hill; "waen" meaning a wagon; "Woden", the Norse God; or even some personal name. The parish was a thinly-populated backwater prior to the building of the first Wanstead House.

[vi] Edward the Confessor, King of England (c.1003-1066: reigned 1042-1066). His reign saw a weakening of royal power in England, and an increase in cultural and political ties with Normandy. Edward was

childless, and the succession dispute following his death ended in the Norman conquest. Edward was canonised in 1161.

vii Ralph fitz Brien was a Domesday tenant of the Bishop of London. His son, Jordan de Brisete, founded priories of St John and St Mary at Clerkenwell during the reign of Stephen.

viii The "Domesday Survey" was carried out over about a year from 1086, when William the Conqueror ordered the land and resources of England to be assessed for taxation. The information collected was recorded in two huge books. The comprehensive nature of the information collected led people to compare it to the Last Judgement. William died before it was fully completed.

ix In England a hundred was the division of a shire for administrative, military and judicial purposes. The name of each hundred was normally that of its customary meeting-place, where local business was transacted and trials took place. The former area of Becontree Hundred now corresponds to the London Boroughs of Newham and Barking and Dagenham and large parts of Waltham Forest and Redbridge. Its early extent also included parts of what is now the London Borough of Havering.

x Since land tenure reforms of the 1920s, the manorial system in England survives only in the form of certain vestigial property rights. However, the manor was for centuries the basic unit of land ownership and local government in rural areas. It was characterised by the vesting of legal power and economic rights in a lord, who was supported from his own direct landholding plus the obligatory contributions of the various categories of tenant under his jurisdiction. These might variously be payable in labour, or produce, or money. The European manorial system has strong analogies to the villa system of the semi-feudalised later Roman Empire, and probably has some of its origins there.

xi A bordar was a person ranking above a serf, but below a villein, in the social hierarchy of the mediaeval countryside. He held just enough land to feed a family and was required to provide labour service on the lord's demesne on specified days of the week.

xii A serf was a person attached to the land owned by a feudal lord and required to perform labour service. He enjoyed minimal legal or customary rights. The status of the serf was hereditary. Serfdom began to decline in the fourteenth century due to the competition for labour following the Black Death. However, the last English serfs were not emancipated until 1574. In Scotland some communities of miners remained in conditions of legal serfdom until the 1790s.

xiii The salt pan is of interest, as Essex was well-known for its salt industry. However, prehistoric, Roman and medieval salterns were concentrated along the coast, and the Wanstead salt pan - on a tidal river - is the county's only known inland salt-works. It is not known precisely where it was located.

xiv The family of Hoding held considerable estates in Essex during the reigns of Henry II and Henry III. The only daughter and heiress of Sir Hugh de Hoding became the second wife of William de Huntercomb, whose first wife was Isabel, daughter and co-heiress of Robert de Muscamp: by her he had Sir Walter de Huntercombe; and, by his wife Alice, his second son, Thomas, born in 1258. Thomas succeeded to his mother's inheritance; and the last of the family holding these estates was John, the son of John, who died in 1383.

xv Sir William de Huntercombe was born in 1221. He died in March 1271 at Huntercombe End, Oxfordshire.

xvi John Tattershall was born at of Well Hall, Eltham, Kent. He married Agnes Chicheley, daughter of John Chicheley, Chamberlain of London, and Margery Knollys, before 1435. He died in 1446.

xvii Sir Ralph Hastings (c.1440-1495). Of Harrowden, Northamptonshire, and Wanstead. Hastings acquired the Wanstead property in right of his second wife, Anne, daughter of John Tattershall. A Yorkist during the Wars of the Roses, he held a variety of offices, of which the most colourful was custodian of the lions and leopards in the Tower of London. His widow sold the property to King Henry VII in 1499, possibly against her will.

xviii Sir Giles Heron (executed 1540). The son of Sir John Heron of Hackney, Treasurer of the Household to both Henry VII and Henry VIII. On his father's death in 1523 Giles became a Ward of Sir Thomas More. He married Cecily, More's daughter, in 1525. Heron's end came after he was overheard 'speaking too freely' of the king. He was convicted of treason and put to death, though whether the evidence supported the charge is considered highly doubtful. His real crimes were his relationship to More and the religious opinions he shared with him. Sir Giles Heron owned the manor of Aldersbrook and was for a time Keeper of Wanstead Park.

xix Sir Thomas More (1478-1535). Lawyer, scholar, polemicist and statesman. More served Henry VIII as Lord Chancellor. He was executed for treason in 1535 after his refusal to take the Oath of Supremacy. More's daughter Cecily was married to Sir Giles Heron, who was also executed in 1540. Thomas More was canonised by the Roman Catholic Church in 1935.

xx Henry VIII, King of England and Lord (later King) of Ireland (1491-1547: reigned 1509-1547). Henry's main political objectives were to centralize the state and augment Royal authority. Though theologically rather conservative and hostile to most Protestant ideas, his desire to set aside his first wife, Catherine of Aragon, and marry again (in order to beget a male heir) set him on a course which ended in his repudiating the authority of the Pope and establishing himself as Supreme Head of the Church in England. Henry was succeeded by Edward VI, the son born to the third of his six wives, Jane Seymour.

xxi The Act of Supremacy of 1534 (26 Hen. 8 c. 1) declared that the King was *"the only supreme head on earth of the Church in England"* and that the English crown should enjoy *"all honours, dignities, pre-eminences, jurisdictions, privileges, authorities, immunities, profits, and commodities to the said dignity."* The Treasons Act 1534 stated that to disavow the Act of Supremacy and to deprive the King of his *"dignity, title, or name"* was to be considered treason.

xxii Richard Rich, 1st Baron Rich (1496/7-1567). Lawyer and statesman, who served Henry VIII, Edward VI and Mary I. Though personally of Catholic sympathies, he took an active role in the dissolution of the monasteries in his capacity as Chancellor of the Court of Augmentation, and greatly profited thereby. Rich was raised to the Peerage in 1548. He was granted the manor of Wanstead in 1549, and built the first Wanstead House.

xxiii Mary I, Queen of England and Ireland (1516-1558: reigned 1553-1558). Mary was the elder daughter of Henry VIII and only surviving child of his first wife, Catherine of Aragon. After succeeding her half-brother, Edward VI, she reversed his radically Protestant settlement of the Church, and re-established Roman Catholicism. Mary married Philip of Habsburg, son of Emperor Charles V, and later King of Spain, but the union was childless. Mary died at 42, possibly from uterine cancer or complications from ovarian cysts. She was succeeded by her half-sister, Elizabeth I, who reinstated the Edwardian reformation in most essentials.

xxiv Edward VI, King of England and Ireland (1537-1553: reigned 1547-1553). The only legitimate son of Henry VIII, by his third wife Jane Seymour. Though he was intellectually precocious, Edward's youth meant that government was largely in the hands of his successive ministers the Dukes of Somerset and Northumberland. His reign saw the Church of England recast on Protestant lines, with a Calvinistic theology balanced by a continuing episcopal structure. At the end of his life Edward attempted to devise the throne by will to his cousin Lady Jane Grey, probably under the influence of Northumberland. However, he was in fact succeeded, after a brief interlude, by his half-sister Mary.

xxv John Dudley, 1st Duke of Northumberland (1504-1553). Soldier and statesman: Lord President of the Council between 1550-1553 in the latter half of Edward VI's reign. His attempt to place his daughter-in-law, Lady Jane Grey, on the throne failed, resulting in his execution when Mary established herself in power.

^{xxvi} Lady Jane Grey (1536/1537-1554). On his deathbed Edward VI amended his will to name his cousin Lady Jane Grey as his successor, bypassing his half-sisters Mary and Elizabeth whom their father Henry VIII had first excluded from the line of succession, and then restored to it (though without removing the question mark over their legitimacy created by the annulment of his marriages to their mothers). Edward's move was, for various reasons, of doubtful legal effect and, as Oliver Dawson states, was suspected of being made under the influence of the Duke of Northumberland. Following Edward's death in 1553, Jane was proclaimed Queen in London, but Mary rallied support and within days had firmly established herself on the throne. Tried and condemned for treason, Jane might yet have been spared, had not Wyatt's rebellion in 1554 made her continued survival seem dangerous. She and her husband were accordingly executed, along with a number of her prominent supporters.

^{xxvii} Robert Rich, 2nd Baron Rich (c.1537-1580). Eldest son and heir of Richard, 1st Baron Rich.

^{xxviii} Robert Dudley, Earl of Leicester (1532-1588). Statesman and close friend of Elizabeth I. Son of John, Duke of Northumberland, and condemned with him for the unsuccessful attempt to place Lady Jane Grey on the throne. He was released in 1554. For many years he was seen as a suitor for the Queen's hand, but the scandal over the death of his first wife Amy Robsart made marriage impossible, assuming Elizabeth had ever seriously considered it. Dudley was raised to the Peerage in 1564.

^{xxix} The speech at Tilbury was delivered in August 1588 by Queen Elizabeth to the soldiers assembled against the expected Spanish invasion. Two versions have survived, of which the following is the more famous: *"...I have always so behaved myself that, under God, I have placed my chiefest strength and safeguard in the loyal hearts and good-will of my subjects; and therefore I am come amongst you, as you see, at this time, not for my recreation and disport, but being resolved, in the midst and heat of the battle, to live and die amongst you all; to lay down for my God, and for my kingdom, and my people, my honour and my blood even, in the dust. I know I have the body but of a weak and feeble woman; but I have the*

heart and stomach of a king, and of a king of England too, and think foul scorn that Parma or Spain, or any prince of Europe, should dare to invade the borders of my realm..."

xxx Sir Philip Sidney (1554-1586). Poet, courtier and soldier. The son of Sir Henry Sidney and Mary, sister of Robert Dudley, earl of Leicester. In 1583, he married Frances, daughter of Sir Francis Walsingham. Sidney died of his wounds after the Battle of Zutphen, in the Netherlands. While lying on the field after being shot, he famously gave his water-bottle to another wounded man, saying *"Thy necessity is yet greater than mine".*

xxxi Amy Robsart (1532-1560). The first wife of Lord Robert Dudley, later Earl of Leicester. After being effectively separated from her husband for some time, she was found dead after apparently falling down a flight of stairs. There were rumours that Dudley had her murdered in order to be free to marry the Queen, though there was no positive evidence of his guilt. However, the scandal ended any possibility of marriage between Elizabeth and Dudley.

xxxii Lettice Knollys, successively Countess of Essex and Leicester (1543-1634). Daughter of Sir William Knollys and Katherine Carey, whose mother, Mary Boleyn, was sister of Queen Elizabeth's mother Anne. However, as Mary had been the principal mistress of Elizabeth's father Henry VIII from about 1520-25, it is not improbable that Lettice's mother and Elizabeth were really half-siblings rather than first cousins. Lettice married Walter Devereux, then Viscount Hertford and later first Earl of Essex, around 1560. She was the mother of Robert Devereux, 2nd Earl of Essex, and Penelope Devereux, later Lady Rich. In 1578 she married secondly Robert Dudley, Earl of Leicester, and thereby earned Queen Elizabeth's undying enmity. After the death of the Earl of Leicester, Lettice married thirdly Sir Christopher Blount, who was executed for treason in 1601.

xxxiii Walter Devereux, 1st Earl of Essex (?1541-1576). Soldier. He attempted to pacify Ulster, expending much of his private fortune to that end, but was eventually recalled. His widow, Lettice, married the Earl of Leicester.

xxxiv Ambrose Dudley, 3rd Earl of Warwick (1528-1590). Soldier and statesman. He was a son of the first Duke of Northumberland, and an elder brother of Robert Dudley, Earl of Leicester. Along with his father and brothers he was implicated in the attempt to place Lady Jane Grey on the throne, and initially condemned to death. Released in 1554, he became Earl of Warwick in 1561 and Queen Elizabeth I employed him in various capacities.

xxxv Sir Christopher Blount (?1565-1601). Probably a cousin of Charles Blount, Earl of Devonshire. He married the mother of Robert, Earl of Essex. Blount was later implicated in Essex's conspiracy against Queen Elizabeth's government and executed.

xxxvi William Cecil, Baron Burghley (1520-1598). Statesman. Served all English monarchs from Henry VIII to Elizabeth I. Chief adviser and minister to Elizabeth I until his death.

xxxvii Catherine Dudley, Countess of Huntingdon (1544-1620). Daughter of John Dudley, 1st Duke of Northumberland and Jane Guilford. She married Henry, 3rd Earl of Huntingdon.

xxxviii Henry Hastings, 3rd Earl of Huntingdon (c.1535-1595). Statesman. His father was an ally of John Dudley, 1st Duke of Northumberland and, in 1553, Henry married Catherine Dudley, Northumberland's daughter. Briefly imprisoned after the failed bid for the throne by Lady Jane Grey, but then pardoned, after which he served Mary I and Elizabeth I loyally. Considered by some as a possible successor to Elizabeth, as he was of Royal Plantagenet descent through his mother.

xxxix Elizabeth Sidney, Countess of Rutland (c.1585-1612). Daughter of Sir Philip Sidney and stepdaughter of Robert, 2nd Earl of Essex. Married Roger Manners, 5th Earl of Rutland, in 1599. The subject of lurid rumours: several sources claim she poisoned Manners to free herself from an unhappy marriage, and was then herself murdered by his family.

xl Roger Manners, 5th Earl of Rutland (1576-1612). Courtier and soldier. In 1599 Manners married Elizabeth Sidney, stepdaughter to the 2nd earl of Essex. The marriage was reportedly not happy, and there were rumours that Elizabeth murdered him. Manners participated in Essex's rebellion against Elizabeth's government, and was heavily fined. Favoured by James I, he was noted by contemporaries for his intellect and talent.

xli Robert Sidney, Earl of Leicester (1563-1626). Statesman and patron of the arts. Brother of Sir Philip Sidney. His mother, Mary, was the sister of Robert Dudley.

xlii Mary Dudley, Lady Sidney (c.1532-1586). Daughter of John, Duke of Northumberland, and sister of Robert, Earl of Leicester. Married Sir Henry Sidney 1551.

xliii Robert Devereux, 2nd Earl of Essex (1565-1601). Sometime favourite of Elizabeth I. An ambitious soldier, he was imprisoned after accusations of entering into a "dishonourable treaty" with the Earl of Tyrone during the Nine Years War in Ireland. He later attempted a coup d'état against Elizabeth's government and was executed for treason.

xliv John Chamberlain (1553-1628). Author of a series of letters written from 1597 to 1626, notable for their literary qualities and value as an historical resource.

xlv Hugh O'Neill, 2nd Earl of Tyrone (c. 1550-1616). Aodh Mór Ó Néill, known as the Great Earl, and heir to Ulster's ancient kings, was once a protégé of the English. However, once installed as chieftain he rebelled against the Tudor Monarchy's assertive policies in Ireland and led Irish resistance during the Nine Years War. Compelled to submit by Lord Mountjoy (later Earl of Devonshire) in 1603, he was lodged at Wanstead before appearing at court, where he was pardoned by James I. However, unable to endure the constraints upon him, and fearful of arrest, he left Ireland in 1607 with the Earl of Tyrconnell in the famous "flight of the Earls". He died in Rome and is buried in the church of San Pietro in Montorio.

^{xlvi} Charles Blount, Earl of Devonshire (1563-1606). 8th Baron Mountjoy until promoted in the Peerage. Soldier. He successfully concluded the Nine Years War in Ireland, using the most ruthless methods. Though implicated in Essex's conspiracy, no action was taken against him. After living with Penelope Devereux "in flagrant adultery", he married her bigamously, as her divorce *a mensa et thoro* from her first husband, Lord Rich, did not permit remarriage. They fell from favour at court in consequence of the scandal.

^{xlvii} The Battle of Zutphen was fought on 22 September 1586, near Zutphen in the Netherlands, between forces of the United Provinces of the Netherlands, aided by the English, against the Spanish. The latter were seeking to suppress the Dutch uprising against the Spanish Crown and restore Catholicism. Though they won this particular engagement, they ultimately failed to re-conquer the United Provinces, which were finally recognised as a state independent of Spain and the Empire in 1648.

^{xlviii} The magnificent Savoy Palace was destroyed during the Peasants' Revolt of 1381. In 1512 a new building was erected on the site, in accordance with the will of Henry VII, as a hospital for the poor. However, this gradually fell into dereliction, was divided into tenements, and finally demolished in the nineteenth century. The Savoy Hotel now occupies part of the site, and only the hospital chapel survives.

^{xlix} Penelope Devereux (died 1607). Daughter of the first Earl of Essex and his wife Lettice Knollys. A noted beauty, she was married against her will to the 3rd Lord Rich but left him for Lord Mountjoy, later Earl of Devonshire, whom she later married bigamously.

^l Robert Rich, 3rd Baron Rich and 1st Earl of Warwick (1559-1618). Son and heir of Robert, 2nd Baron Rich. Married Lady Penelope Devereux, who left him and whom he divorced *a mensa et thoro* in 1605. Shortly before his death he was promoted in the Peerage as Earl of Warwick.

li Thomas Howard, Earl of Suffolk (1561-1626). Admiral and statesman. A son of Thomas Howard, 4th Duke of Norfolk. He took as his second wife Katherine Knyvet, widow of Richard, a son of Robert Rich, 2nd Baron Rich.

lii Mountjoy Blount, 1st Earl of Newport (c. 1597-1666). The natural son of Charles Blount, Earl of Devonshire, and Penelope Devereux. Courtier, official and soldier. Raised to the Peerage in his own right 1627. His three surviving sons were all described as "idiots" and, after each in turn died without issue, the title became extinct in 1679.

liii James I and VI (1566 -1625). Reigned as James VI, King of Scots, from 1567 to 1625; and King of England and Ireland as James I from 1603 to 1625. He succeeded his mother Mary upon her abdication when he was thirteen months old, and did not gain full control of his government until 1581. His succession to the throne of England on the death of Elizabeth I united the crowns of the two kingdoms, though union of the parliaments followed only in 1707. James was succeeded by his second son, Charles I.

liv Sir Roger Aston (died 1612) was Gentleman of the Bedchamber and Master of the Great Wardrobe under James I.

lv Robert Cecil, 1st Earl of Salisbury (1563?-1612), son of William Cecil, 1st Baron Burghley and Mildred Cooke. Succeeded his father as chief minister to Elizabeth I, and retained his position under James I, who raised him to the Peerage.

lvi Christian IV of Denmark-Norway (born 1577: reigned 1588-1648) is to date the longest-reigning Danish monarch. He was brother-in-law to James I, who was married to his sister Anne.

lvii Dr. Jonas Carisius was Danish Ambassador to England 1610-11.

lviii Sir Dudley Carleton, later 1st Viscount Dorchester (1573-1632) was a diplomat and Secretary of State 1628-32.

lix Sir Edward Phellips, or Phelips (c1555/60-1614) was a lawyer and politician. Of a family that had risen from yeoman status, he became

Speaker of the House of Commons from 1604 until 1611, and subsequently Master of the Rolls from 1611. He commissioned the building of Montacute House, in Somerset.

lx Henry Howard, Earl of Northampton (1540-1614) Courtier. A crypto-Catholic, Northampton was distinguished for his learning and charitable bequests, though his religious views brought him periods of Royal disfavour. At the end of his life he was implicated in the poisoning of Sir Thomas Overbury by his great-niece Lady Frances Howard, already notorious for her marital misadventures.

lxi Robert Carr (c.1587-1645) 1st Viscount Rochester (from 1611) and 1st Earl of Somerset (from 1613). Courtier and intimate favourite of King James I. Married the notorious Lady Frances Howard, and implicated with her in the poisoning of Sir Thomas Overbury.

lxii George Villiers, 1st Duke of Buckingham (1592-1628). Influential but widely unpopular favourite of King James I and his son Charles I. He was murdered by a disgruntled army officer who believed he had been unjustly passed over for promotion.

lxiii John Boteler (c.1565/7-1637), 1st Baronet of Hatfield Woodhall in the County of Hertford from 1620, Baron Boteler of Brantfield in the County of Hertford, from 1628. Served as Member of Parliament for Hertfordshire from 1625 to 1626.

lxiv Charles I, King of England, Scotland and Ireland (1600-1649: reigned 1625-1649). His religious policies, unsuccessful foreign initiatives and attempts to rule without an increasingly assertive Parliament aroused fierce opposition, culminating in the civil wars of 1642-1648. Following the second civil war the purged "Rump Parliament" tried Charles as a "tyrant, traitor, murderer and public enemy" and condemned him to death. A "commonwealth", or republic, was then established which lasted until 1660.

lxv Francis Bacon, Viscount St Albans and Baron Verulam (1561-1626). Statesman, lawyer, philosopher and scientist.

lxvi Sir Henry Mildmay (1593-1664). Member of Parliament variously for Maldon and Westbury between 1620 and 1660. He was present at the trial of Charles I and a member of the Councils of State between 1649 and 1652. Attempted escape in 1660 when called on to account for the Crown Jewels, which had been in his custody. Sentenced to life imprisonment as a regicide, and died in custody.

lxvii Sir Francis Walsingham (c.1532-1590). Statesman, and one of Elizabeth I's inner circle of advisers. Involved in various aspects of foreign, domestic and religious policy. He set up a highly efficient intelligence network.

lxviii William Halliday (c.1565-1624) was not, as Dawson styles him, a knight. A wealthy merchant, apparently born in Gloucestershire, he was involved in the East India Company, of which his cousin Sir Leonard had been a founder. Elected as a director in 1616, he became Governor in 1621. In April 1619, after *"long and ernest sollicitation"* by the Marquess (later Duke) of Buckingham, who was acting on instructions from King James, he married off his daughter Anne to Sir Henry Mildmay.

lxix The East India Company was a joint-stock company that was granted an Royal Charter by Elizabeth I in 1600. The oldest among several similarly formed European East India Companies, the East India Company came after 1757 to rule large swathes of India, exercising military power and assuming administrative functions under the increasingly fictitious suzerainty of the Timurid (Mughal) Emperors, whose power declined steadily throughout the eighteenth century. The Company's political role gradually eclipsed its original commercial objectives. Company rule lasted until 1858 when, following the "Indian Mutiny", the Crown assumed the direct administration of India.

lxx Shortly after the restoration of Charles II, Parliament passed "An Act of Free and General Pardon, Indemnity, and Oblivion". This was to give legal force to the King's guarantee given in the Declaration of Breda that punishment for actions committed during the civil wars and Commonwealth would be limited to those most directly concerned in the death of his father Charles I. He left it to Parliament to decide what this was to mean in detail. The debate on the Bill continued for several weeks, and the list of those who were to be excepted from pardon underwent a succession of amendments. The persons principally under consideration were the Commissioners summoned to sit in judgement at the King's trial and, in particular, those who signed his death warrant. However, a number of other officials who were concerned in the trial or execution in other capacities were also considered, as well as Hugh Peters, a republican preacher who had sought to justify it. The trials which followed the Act saw 13 individuals executed, while a further nineteen were sentenced to life imprisonment. Others were pardoned by exercise of the Royal Prerogative or escaped abroad.

[lxxi] Edward Conway, 1st Viscount Conway (1564-1631). Soldier and statesman. Secretary of State 1623-8.

[lxxii] Sir Nicholas Coote (died 1633), a member of the local gentry, lived at Valence House, in Dagenham. The last of Dagenham's five ancient manor houses to survive, Valence House is preserved as a museum.

[lxxiii] Probably Sir John Smith, of Bidborough, Kent, who was married to Lady Isabel Rich, a relative both of Lord Newport and Lord Holland.

[lxxiv] Henry Rich, 1st Earl of Holland (1590-1649). Courtier and soldier. The son of Robert Rich, 1st Earl of Warwick and of Penelope Devereux, Lady Rich, and the younger brother of Robert Rich, 2nd Earl of Warwick. Rich was created Earl of Holland in 1624. He was beheaded in 1649 after being tried by the victorious Parliamentarians for treason, having deserted to the Royalist camp during the Civil Wars.

[lxxv] "Ship money" was a mediaeval tax revived by Charles I during his attempt to rule without Parliament. Charles had obtained legal opinions that ship money could be imposed by writ under the Great Seal without the consent of Parliament. In former times, the tax had only applied to coastal

towns in time of war. However, the collection of the tax inland during peacetime started in 1634. Initially the tax achieved its objective, and Charles' government was able, from this and other sources of revenue, to finance ordinary domestic expenditure without summoning Parliament. However, it provoked increasing resistance and by 1639 less than 20% of the sums demanded were being paid. Ship money was abolished by the Long Parliament.

lxxvi Sir Edward Nicholas (1593-1669) held a variety of offices, including that of Secretary of State to Charles I 1641-1649. He was disliked by the Queen Dowager Henrietta Maria and, for a time, was out of favour with the exiled Charles II. However, he was restored as Secretary of State in 1654 and held this position until his retirement in 1662.

lxxvii Charles II, King of England, Scotland and Ireland (1630-1685: nominally succeeded his father 1649, effective reign 1660-1685). Charles returned from exile in 1660 following the collapse of the Commonwealth. He substantially restored Royal authority while weathering several major crises. However, his desire to minimise his dependence on Parliament led him to a state of political subservience toward France in exchange for subsidies. He died without legitimate issue, and was succeeded by his politically inept brother James II, formerly Duke of York.

lxxviii Cornelius Holland (1599-c.1671). Member of Parliament from 1642. Holland is alleged to have been the chief hand in drawing up the charges against King Charles I. Wanted at the Restoration as a regicide, he fled to Switzerland and died at Lausanne.

lxxix Nicholas Love (1608-82). Member of Parliament from 1645. Participated in drawing up the charges against the King. In 1660, with the Restoration imminent, Love feared prosecution as a regicide and fled to Hamburg, eventually moving to Vevey in Switzerland, where he died.

lxxx After the establishment of the Commonwealth in 1649, most of the coronation regalia, some of which dated back to the Saxon period, were melted down or dispersed. Upon the restoration of Charles II in 1660, the lost items had to be replaced. The only intact earlier pieces to survive are three swords and one spoon, though some individual gems were retrieved and have been reincorporated in the modern Crown Jewels.

lxxxi Samuel Pepys (1633-1703). An able and reforming Chief Secretary to the Admiralty under Charles II and James II. Now chiefly remembered for his vivid and revealing diary.

lxxxii James, Duke of York, later King James II of England and Ireland and James VII of Scotland (1633-1701: effective reign 1685-1688). James succeeded his brother Charles II in 1685. He quickly alienated the political class by his obstinacy, insensitivity, autocratic tendencies and pro-French and pro-Catholic policies. A Dutch invasion led by his son-in-law William, Prince of Orange, met with little opposition (William was the husband of James' elder daughter, Mary, by his first wife Anne Hyde). James fled the country in December 1688 and was deemed by Parliament to have abdicated. His subsequent attempt at securing a restoration via Ireland, where his loyal viceroy Lord Tyrconnell had largely retained control, was unsuccessful. Parliament, ignoring all constitutional precedent and invoking some highly dubious pretexts, passed over James' son, the infant Prince of Wales, and offered the throne to the Prince and Princess of Orange as joint sovereigns, subject to their acceptance of limitations on their power.

lxxxiii Sir Robert Brookes. Highly regarded Member of Parliament for Aldborough in Suffolk. Purchased the Wanstead estate in 1661 from James, Duke of York (later King James II), who had been granted it after its confiscation from Sir Henry Mildmay. Brookes, who was Mildmay's son-in-law, and held it until his mysterious death by drowning in 1669.

lxxxiv John Berkeley, 1st Baron Berkeley of Stratton (1602-1678) was a royalist soldier. From 1648 he was closely associated with James, Duke of York (later King James II), and after the Restoration rose to some prominence. According to Lord Clarendon, he was notorious for spinning incredible tales of his exploits. Clarendon wrote that through constant re-telling he may have come to believe them himself.

lxxxv The Hon. Henry Brouncker, later 3rd Viscount Brouncker (c.1627-1688). Courtier, who served as Cofferer of the Household to Charles II, and Gentleman of the Bedchamber to James, Duke of York (later King James II). Samuel Pepys called Brouncker: *"a pestilent rogue, an atheist, that would have sold his king and country for sixpence, almost"*. Though debauched and frivolous, he was not without intelligence and was a noted chess player. His elder brother William, 2nd Viscount Brouncker, was a famous mathematician and first President of the Royal Society.

lxxxvi Charles Berkeley (1630-1665), second son of Sir Charles Berkeley I who later, by special remainder, succeeded him as 2nd Viscount Fitzhardinge. Groom of the bedchamber to the Duke of York 1656-62; keeper of the privy purse 1662. Knighted 30 May 1660; created Viscount Fitzhardinge of Berehaven 14 July 1663 and Earl of Falmouth 17 March 1665. Killed on board the Royal Charles in the battle of Southwold Bay on 3 June 1665. He pandered to the vices of the King and his brother, but was said by Bishop Burnet to be *"a young man of no extraordinary parts, but of a generous and noble disposition"*.

lxxxvii Sir William Penn (1621-1670). Admiral, and father of William Penn, founder of Pennsylvania. Penn served the Commonwealth, but seems also to have been in contact with exiled Royalists. He actively supported the restoration of Charles II.

lxxxviii Sir Josiah Child, 1st Baronet (1630-1699). Second son of a London merchant, the formidable and ruthless Child became Governor of the East India Company and acquired an immense fortune. Author of the influential *Brief Observations concerning Trade* and the *Interest of Money* (1668), and *A New Discourse of Trade* (1668 and 1690). He purchased the Wanstead estate in 1673. He seems to have done little to the house, but spent prodigious sums on landscaping the park and its surroundings. Married three times, Josiah Child had eight known children. He was succeeded briefly in the baronetcy by his elder surviving son Josiah II, from whom he was estranged, and then by his younger son and principal heir Richard, later ennobled as 1st Earl Tylney of Castlemaine.

[lxxxix] Sir John Child (died 1690). Governor of Bombay. Involved the Company in an unsuccessful war with the Mughal Emperor Aurangzeb. Charged at the end of his life with "tyrannical conduct" and "want of faith with natives". Often incorrectly identified as brother to Josiah Child, it seems unlikely that they were related at all: not only does it appear that their fathers had different names, but their armorial bearings were dissimilar. There seems to be no doubt that Sir Josiah did have a brother named John, but he has been identified with an individual who died in London in 1686.

[xc] Sir Francis Child the elder (1642-1713). Goldsmith, banker. Variously Member of Parliament for the City of London, Alderman and Lord Mayor. He appears to have had no relationship to Sir Josiah Child, though the two families used the same armorial bearings.

[xci] John Evelyn (1620-1706). A writer, gardener and diarist, Evelyn helped found the Royal Society.

[xcii] The elder Sir Josiah Child's daughter Rebecca (died 1712) married Charles Somerset, Marquis of Worcester, heir to the 1st Duke of Beaufort, in 1682. Their son Henry succeeded his grandfather in 1700 as 2nd Duke of Beaufort.

[xciii] Dawson is not quite correct to say that Sir Josiah II succeeded his father at Wanstead. Josiah (c.1668-1704) latterly became estranged from his father who, at his death in 1699, bequeathed him no more than the £4,000 per annum which had been settled upon him at marriage. It was Josiah's younger half-brother Richard who was designated their father's principal heir, at the age of 19. Josiah II was Member of Parliament for Wareham between 1702 and 1704. He died without issue, and was succeeded in the baronetcy by Richard.

[xciv] Richard Child, later Tylney, 1st Earl Tylney of Castlemaine (1680-1750). A younger son of Sir Josiah Child, he inherited Wanstead in 1699 as his elder half-brother Josiah II was out of favour with their father. In 1704 Josiah II died, and Richard also succeeded him as 3rd baronet, reuniting

the family fortune and bringing his annual income to some £10,000.
Richard Child variously represented Maldon and Essex in the House of
Commons for most of the period between 1705 and 1734. In 1715, after
several years of solicitation, he succeeded in purchasing his ennoblement
via the King's mistress Melusine von der Schulenburg, Duchess of Munster
(afterwards Kendal). He was gazetted in 1718 as Viscount of Castlemaine in
the County of Kerry and Baron of Newtown in the County of Donegal, and
promoted in the Irish Peerage as Earl Tylney of Castlemaine in 1731. The
Child family had no known connection with Ireland, but Irish peerages
were often used as consolation prizes for men who were considered
unsuitable or unready for their British equivalents. In 1733, Child assumed
the surname Tylney by Act of Parliament, to comply with the terms of an
inheritance from his wife's uncle Frederick Tylney. Richard Child was
responsible for commissioning the new, Palladian, Wanstead House, which
was begun around 1715 and completed by 1722. The gardens were also
radically reordered in his time, in at least two major phases of work. The
lake system as it now exists was largely his creation. Of his nine known
children, only one - Emma – left legitimate issue, by her husband Robert
Long. Their son James inherited Wanstead in 1784.

xcv Colen Campbell (1676-1729). Influential Palladian architect. Campbell
published *Vitruvius Britannicus or the British Architect*. Apart from
Wanstead House, major commissions included Burlington House,
Houghton Hall, Stourhead, and Rolls House in Chancery Lane.

xcvi Dawson's contention that "the gardens were destroyed at the wreckage
of the house" is rather too sweeping. Wanstead Park remains a nationally
important historic landscape, as reflected by its Grade II* listing, and
preserves many features from the late 17th to the early 19th centuries.
Wanstead Park's modern landscape began its evolution when the estate
was bought by Sir Josiah Child in 1673. He laid out great avenues and
plantations of trees to the north, south and west of the house, as well as
creating a pair of lakes which were later joined to become The Basin.
George London extended and elaborated the gardens in a formal baroque
style for Sir Josiah's son, Richard (later 1st Earl Tylney), probably at some

time in the latter half of the period 1699-1714. London's design was heavily modified 1715-45 in line with changing fashions, though the skeleton of London's layout was retained. Most significantly, an extensive lake system was created around three sides of the park, from which five of the original nine largest water bodies still survive. Regionally important nurseryman and landscape gardener Adam Holt was certainly active in this phase of work, and involvement by William Kent and Charles Bridgeman has been suggested. Further softening of the landscape were carried out by the 2nd Earl (1750-84), including modifications to the lakes, and Wanstead Park assumed its mature appearance. The Temple and Grotto were also built in the 2nd Earl's time. Following several decades in which the estate was not regularly used by its owners, and some features were lost, there was a brief revival after the marriage of William and Catherine Pole-Tylney-Long-Wellesley in 1812. Advice was obtained from Humphry Repton and Lawrence Kennedy, and selectively implemented, before the landscape fell into abandonment and decay after demolition of the house in the 1820s. Despite the loss of thousands of mature trees, sold for timber in the 1820s and 1830s, the outlines of the wooded and grassland areas of the park remain recognisable from the final phase of the gardens, as do the lakes.

[xcvii] Dawson is incorrect in attributing The Grotto to Richard, 1st Earl Tylney. Construction actually commenced around 1760 in the time of his son, John, the 2nd Earl. The building was intended to replace the earlier 'Barge House' at the southern extremity of the Ornamental Water, and comprised a boathouse at its lower level, with a room furnished for entertainment above. It also included accommodation for a keeper or servant. Documentary evidence suggests that the building was complete by 1763, though it was subject to some remodelling in 1781. As Dawson states elsewhere, it was burned down in 1884, and not rebuilt. Little more than the façade now survives, though this continues to provide an important focus for views from the eastern side of the Ornamental Water.

[xcviii] The lake in question, The Basin, is actually an irregular octagon. Jan Kip's imaginary aerial view of Wanstead to the west, from around 1715, shows a pair of semi-circular fish-ponds flanking the main drive to the west

of Wanstead House, each with an island in the centre. However, by 1722 The Basin had been remodelled into its present form, as a single lake, with the drive being diverted round it.

[xcix] John Child, later Tylney, 2nd Earl Tylney of Castlemaine (1712-1784). Born a younger son - rather than grandson, as Dawson incorrectly states - of Richard, 1st Earl Tylney, John succeeded to his father's titles in 1750 as two older brothers had predeceased him. He made significant changes to Wanstead Park, continuing the process begun under his father of softening the earlier formal layout of the gardens. He was responsible for constructing the Temple and the Grotto. A frequent visitor to the Continent, the Earl went abroad permanently in 1763, by some accounts to escape prosecution for an "unnatural crime" he had committed at Wanstead. He spent most of the remainder of his life living in Florence and Naples. By many reports a good-natured and generous man, the 2nd Earl never married and the family titles became extinct on his death, with the Wanstead estate passing to his cousin Sir James Long.

[c] Sir James Tylney-Long (1736-1794). Landowner and Member of Parliament. Born James Long, (later Sir James Long, 7th baronet) he inherited the Wanstead estate in 1784 from his uncle, the 2nd Earl Tylney, and took the additional name of Tylney. Though he seems to have visited Wanstead only very rarely, he largely paid for the rebuilding of the parish church.

[ci] Horace Walpole (1717-1797), later 4th Earl of Orford, was son of the Prime Minister Sir Robert Walpole. An antiquarian, aesthete and man of letters, he was acquainted with John, 2nd Earl Tylney, and part of the same social circle, many members of which were homosexual. Walpole's own private life remains mysterious, though he never married.

[cii] Catherine Tylney-Long (1789-1825). Daughter and heiress of Sir James Tylney-Long. In 1812 she married William, son of William Wellesley-Pole, later fourth Earl of Mornington, to her subsequent great misfortune. Their married name became Pole-Tylney-Long-Wellesley (though they used Long-Wellesley informally).

ciii Prince of Condé (1736-1818). Louis Joseph de Bourbon was Prince of Condé from 1740 to his death. A member of a cadet branch of the French Royal House, he left France in 1789 following the outbreak of revolution and returned only at the restoration of Louis XVIII in 1814. He rented Wanstead House 1802-1810 *"at the princely price of £350 a year"*. The Condé line became extinct with the death of the Prince's son in 1830, the only heir to the title, his grandson the Duc d'Enghien, having notoriously been kidnapped and shot on Napoleon Bonaparte's orders in 1804 (a decision which shocked European opinion and of which Joseph Fouché famously said *"It was worse than a crime; it was a blunder"*).

civ Louis XVIII, King of France and Navarre (1755-1824: nominally succeeded his nephew 1795, effective reign 1814-1824). The younger brother of Louis XVI, Louis Stanislas, Comte de Provence, as he was then styled, left France in 1791 during the revolution. From 1793-1795 the late king's son Louis Charles was regarded by royalists as Louis XVII, though he never reigned (he was a prisoner in Paris with his parents and other members of the deposed Royal Family from 1792 until his death). Louis Stanislas returned to France only in 1814 when the Bourbon Monarchy was restored in his person. Louis was childless, and was disastrously succeeded by his reactionary and politically inept younger brother, the Comte d'Artois, as Charles X.

cv William Pole-Tylney-Long-Wellesley, 4th Earl of Mornington (1788-1857). Born William Wellesley Pole, he married Catherine Tylney-Long, heiress to the Wanstead estate, in 1812. Having decided to use Wanstead House as their principal residence, William and Catherine felt that the house and its gardens required significant refurbishment. However, while the desirability of undertaking improvements offers some mitigation for the calamities which followed, there can be no doubt that William was wildly extravagant. He squandered his interest in his wife's inheritance in less than a decade, and repeatedly ran up enormous debts. Their initially happy marriage deteriorated, and Catherine later hinted that she had been infected by her husband with venereal disease before he eventually abandoned her for another woman, Helena Paterson-Bligh. Catherine died aged 36 in 1825, two years after Wanstead House was demolished for the value of its building materials (the Wanstead estate, being tied up in trusts, was beyond the creditors' reach). As Dawson mentions, William then married Mrs Paterson-Bligh, whose fortune he also rapidly dissipated before abandoning her in turn. He spent his last years subsisting on a small pension from his kinsman the Duke of Wellington. The *Morning Chronicle* obituary of Lord Mornington, as he had by then become, read: *"Redeemed by no single virtue, adorned by no single grace, his life has gone out without even a flicker of repentance; his 'retirement' was that of one who was deservedly avoided by all men."* William Pole-Tylney-Long-Wellesley was Member of Parliament at various times for St Ives, Wiltshire, and Essex. From 1842 he was styled Viscount Wellesley, and succeeded his father as Earl of Mornington in 1845. He and Catherine had three children, who all reached adulthood, but none of them married or had issue.

[cvi] The Prince Adolphus, 1st Duke of Cambridge (1774-1850), was the tenth child and seventh son of George III and Queen Charlotte. He held the title of Duke of Cambridge from 1801, and served as Viceroy of Hanover on behalf of his brothers George IV and William IV.

[cvii] A member of the local gentry, Lady Smith-Burges(s) was born Margaret Burges in 1744. Her family were Lords of the Manor of East Ham during the eighteenth and nineteenth centuries. Married twice, latterly - at the age of 72 - to John, 4th Earl Poulett (which elicited some unkind comments). She died in Brighton in 1828.

[cviii] William Pole-Tylney-Long-Wellesley had only a limited life interest in his wife's estate so, despite his "tremendous and complicated debts", a large part of her inheritance was preserved for their children.

[cix] Although Dawson presents the destruction of Wanstead House as a traumatic experience for Catherine Pole-Tylney-Long-Wellesley, there seems to be little evidence that she felt any deep attachment to it. Her father had rarely visited Wanstead, much preferring the Long family's traditional seat at Draycott Cerne. Catherine seems only to have resided at Wanstead for long periods in the years after 1810; and the sale of the

contents and fabric of the house does not appear to have been resisted by her.

cx George Henry Robins (1777-1847). Auctioneer. According to Walter Thornbury in *Old and New London*, Robins was "...one of the most eloquent auctioneers who ever wielded an ivory hammer. The Auction Mart stood opposite the Rotunda of the Bank. It is said that Robins was once offered £2,000 and all his expenses to go and dispose of a valuable property in New York. His annual income was guessed at £12,000. It is said that half the landed property in England had passed under his hammer. Robins, "with incomparable powers of blarney and soft sawder, wrote poetical and alluring advertisements (attributed by some to eminent literary men), which were irresistibly attractive".

cxi William and Catherine Pole-Tylney-Long-Wellesley actually had three children, rather than two as stated by Dawson: William, later 5th Earl of Mornington (1813-1863); James (1815-1851) and Victoria (1819-1897). In the years following their mother's death, the children were the subject of a sordid custody battle between their father and their mother's two unmarried sisters, Dorothy and Emma, who were caring for them. Their uncle, the Duke of Wellington, successfully took legal action on their behalf to restrain their father and protect their inheritance from his depredations. Following Lady Victoria's death, her Goddaughter Octavia Barry wrote *Lady Victoria Pole Tylney Long Wellesley: a Memoir* which, though pious in tone and discreet in relation to the disasters Lady Victoria's family had suffered, contains some useful information.

cxii Helena Paterson (1794-1869). Married, firstly, Captain Thomas Bligh, following which she was known by the name of "Paterson-Bligh"; and secondly, in 1828, following an adulterous affair of several years duration, William Pole-Tylney-Long-Wellesley. The latter abandoned Helena in the 1830s, leaving her virtually destitute to the extent that, at times, she was reputedly forced to live on parish relief.

cxiii Arthur Wellesley, 1st Duke of Wellington (1769-1852). A renowned soldier, Wellington was responsible for the final defeat of Napoleon

Bonaparte at the Battle of Waterloo in 1815. He was also an important, though less successful, Tory statesman. He was Prime Minister from 1828-30 and (briefly as a caretaker) in 1834.

cxiv William Pole-Tylney-Long-Wellesley was indeed unsuccessful in the 1813 court case concerning his attempts to close Wanstead Park, but later achieved his objective via a private Act of Parliament. However, showing a degree of magnanimity in victory, he paid for the road skirting the park to be upgraded, and allowed public access to Wanstead Park at specified times.

cxv Henry Wellesley, 1st Earl Cowley (1804-1884). Diplomat. His father was the youngest brother of the 1st Duke of Wellington. Cowley's cousin, the 5th Earl of Mornington, had originally made a will bequeathing all his estates to his only surviving sibling Lady Victoria, who intended to return them to the Long family upon her decease. However, Lord Mornington unexpectedly made another will three weeks before his death in 1863, by which he left all his landed property - including Wanstead Park - to Lord Cowley.

cxvi Wanstead Golf Club is housed in a group of 18th century buildings, now much altered, around a courtyard. These were once stables and outhouses for Wanstead House.

cxvii The history of The Temple is not well documented. It is known that William Chambers designed a garden temple for John, 2nd Earl Tylney of Castlemaine, around 1753 when they met in Florence, which was *"proposed to be executed in his Lordship's gardens at Wanstead"*. The design was apparently not used, but a garden temple was indeed subsequently constructed as an eye-catcher at the end of a pre-existing avenue which was truncated some 250m from the Heronry Pond. The date is not known, though the extant building is assumed to be roughly contemporary with The Grotto. The architect is likewise unknown, though the central portion does bear some superficial resemblance to a larger garden temple, also probably designed by William Chambers, at Gunnersbury Park. The Temple was extended in two phases and was later used as keepers' accommodation. It has been suggested that The Temple was originally constructed to house the "menagerie" (probably more accurately described as an exotic aviary), mentioned by Jérôme Lalande in his "Diary of a Trip to England" of 1763.

cxviii The refreshment chalet was a late 19th century wooden refreshment pavilion, positioned to the west of the Temple, and destroyed by fire in 1950.

cxix Prince Arthur, Duke of Connaught and Strathearn (1850-1942) was third son and seventh child of Queen Victoria. He later served as the Governor General of Canada.

cxx Victoria, Queen of the United Kingdom of Great Britain and Ireland (1819-1901: reigned 1837-1901). Born Princess Alexandrina Victoria, she was the only child of Prince Edward, Duke of Kent and Strathearn, the fourth son and fifth child of George III, and Princess Victoria of Saxe-Coburg-Saalfeld. In 1876, she assumed the additional title of Empress of India.

cxxi The poet Alexander Pope (1688-1744) moved to a villa at Twickenham in 1719, where he created his famous garden. As this was separated from his house by a public road, be obtained permission to create a tunnel to it from his basement, which was enlarged into a grotto with several chambers which he decorated with geological specimens, shells, mirrors and so forth. This drew some mockery but also much emulation; and it was the ancestor of many similar garden structures. Though a denuded shadow of its former self, Pope's grotto still survives, and is occasionally opened to the public.

cxxii Oliver Dawson's "French landscape gardener named Roche" was in fact the celebrated cartographer John (originally Jean) Rocque (f.1709-1762). His parents, who are assumed to have been French Huguenot émigrés, settled in London by about 1709. Rocque worked as a surveyor, engraver, cartographer and map-seller. In addition, he was involved in garden design with his brother Bartholomew, a landscape gardener.

cxxiii The most important surviving features of Wanstead Park's eighteenth century landscape are its lakes. Extensive though they are - totalling some 43 acres in size - they are merely the remnant of a waterscape which was once considerably larger. Of the nine significant water bodies created between 1715 and 1745, only five now survive: The Basin; Shoulder of Mutton Pond; Heronry Pond; Perch Pond; and the Ornamental Water. The others - the Great Lake, the Reservoir, the Lake Pond, and the Square Pond - were abandoned in the first half of the nineteenth century. The reasons for this are not explicitly documented, but clues on maps from the period suggest it was a result of inadequate inflow and/or leakage. The lack of a resident owner at Wanstead House between about 1763 and 1810 may also have resulted in a lack of maintenance of the system which was later judged too difficult or expensive to reverse. Since 1900 these problems have been exacerbated by residential development of much of the park's former water catchment area and associated drainage schemes.

cxxiv Valens (Flavius Julius Valens), Roman Emperor (328-378: reigned 364-378). Appointed co-emperor by his brother Valentinian I and allocated the eastern half of the empire. Valens was regarded as less able than the formidable Valentinian. Nonetheless, he was "a conscientious administrator, careful of the interests of the humble". He was killed in battle against the Goths near Adrianople in Thrace, along with most of his field army. This calamity crippled the empire militarily for decades.

cxxv Constantine I (Flavius Valerius Aurelius Constantinus), Roman Emperor (c.270-337: reigned 306-337). Proclaimed *Augustus* by the soldiers at York in 306, following the death there of his father Constantius I. Constantine was initially recognised by Galerius, Senior Tetrarch, only as *Caesar* (or junior emperor), with authority over Britain, Gaul and Spain. However, by 324 he had eliminated his rivals and established sole rule over the Roman world. Constantine introduced economic and administrative innovations, adapting and building upon the reforms of Diocletian. He re-founded Byzantium as Constantinopolis, the modern Istanbul. He first legalised, then established a leading role for, Christianity, being himself baptised on his death-bed.

[cxxxvi] Smart Lethieullier (1701-1760). Lord of the Manor of Aldersbrook and noted antiquarian. Lethieullier wrote four letters describing or mentioning the Roman antiquities discovered in Wanstead Park during landscaping works between 1715 and 1746. He stated that remains of Roman buildings had been visible in at least two locations in the park, describing the discovery of a tessellated pavement and other antiquities. The occasion of the discoveries was the massive landscaping schemes commissioned by Richard Child, later first Earl Tylney. Lethieullier was eye-witness to some of the finds, and described others at second hand. No other account of these remains seems to have survived, and all visible trace of Roman structures was "obliterated" during the course of the works. Oliver Dawson's account closely paraphrases elements of Lethieullier's letters. Archaeological work from the 1960s to the present has shed some light on Roman – and prehistoric – settlement in Wanstead Park, but the location of the Roman building containing the pavement has not yet been definitively established.

[cxxvii] By the second half of the nineteenth century Epping Forest was coming under increasing pressure from landowners who wished to enclose it for development. This was resisted by the commoners, who had rights to graze their animals and cut timber. They obtained the aid of the Corporation of London, which obtained an injunction to throw open some 3,000 acres that had been enclosed in the preceding 20 years. In 1875 and 1876, the Corporation bought a further 3,000 acres of open waste land. Under the Epping Forest Act 1878, which gave force to the recommendations of a commission appointed under earlier Acts, the forest was "disafforested", meaning that forest law was no longer applicable to it, and the Corporation was appointed as its custodian. The 1878 Act transformed Epping Forest into a public open space. Wanstead Park is managed as part of Epping Forest, though the park proper has its own bylaws. The Corporation acquired it separately from the rest of the forest by purchase from the Earl of Cowley, a member of the Wellesley family, in 1882.

[cxxviii] John T. Bedford (1813-1900). Author and journalist. Member of the Court of Common Council of the City of London. In 1871 Bedford helped

initiate the fight to save Epping Forest as an open space. He wrote whimsical pieces on local themes for *The London Charivari*, later *Punch*, under the pseudonym "Robert the Waiter".

cxxix City of London Cemetery. By the mid-19th century churchyards within the City of London were becoming overcrowded, unsanitary and unfit to be used for further burials. To answer the problem the Corporation purchased 90 acres of farm land at Little Ilford in 1854. Formerly the larger part of Aldersbrook Manor, the property had once been owned by the family of Smart Lethieullier. The first burial at the City of London Cemetery took place in June 1856. The cemetery contains re-interments from demolished City churches, including the bodies of some luminaries of former times such as Robert Hooke, the scientist (1635-1703).

cxxx Sir George Jessel (1824-1883). One of the most influential commercial law and equity judges of his time, he served as the Master of the Rolls.

cxxxi Sir William Harcourt (1827-1904) was a lawyer, writer and Liberal statesman. He served as Member of Parliament and held the offices of Home Secretary and Chancellor of the Exchequer under W E Gladstone before becoming, briefly, Leader of the Opposition.

cxxxii Parish Church of St Mary the Virgin, Wanstead. There was a church at Wanstead by 1208. The ancient parish church, which stood about 70 feet south of the present one, was a small and humble structure. Unsatisfactorily enlarged and renovated in 1709-10, by the end of the century it had become inadequate for the needs of the growing parish and was replaced by the existing building. The new church was made possible by the generosity of Sir James Tylney-Long, who donated the ground on which it was built and defrayed a large part of the cost of construction. Designed by Thomas Hardwick, it was completed in 1790, and dedicated in 1791. In its style, materials and construction it echoes the nearby Wanstead House. At the time of writing it is the only Grade I listed building in the London Borough of Redbridge, and retains much of its original character.

^{cxxxiii} The Reverend Samuel Glasse (1734-1812) was a theologian, advocate of Sunday schools, and a chaplain to the king. He was Rector of Wanstead from 1786.

^{cxxxiv} John Saltmarsh (died 1647). Born in Yorkshire, a radical religious controversialist and preacher. Originally a Minister in the Established Church, he became a chaplain in the army. Came to be considered one of the "Seekers". William Haller called him "that strange genius, part poet and part whirling dervish".

^{cxxxv} The Reverend James Pound (1669-1724). Presented to the rectory of Wanstead by Sir Richard Child in 1707, having previously been a medical chaplain in the service of the East India Company. Sir Isaac Newton described him as "the best astronomer in Europe".

^{cxxxvi} Sir Isaac Newton (1643-1727). Physicist, mathematician, astronomer and natural philosopher. His *Philosophiæ Naturalis Principia Mathematica* is considered to be among the most influential books in the history of science.

^{cxxxvii} Maypole dancing was prohibited by an ordinance of the Long Parliament in 1644 as *"a Heathenish vanity, generally abused to superstition and wickedness."* However, it was revived after the restoration of the Monarchy in 1660. The largest maypole ever recorded was erected at that time in the Strand, near the site of the present church of St Mary-le-Strand. This was over a hundred and thirty feet tall, and stood until blown over by a high wind in 1672, after which it was moved to Wanstead and served as a mount for a telescope.

^{cxxxviii} The Reverend James Bradley (1693-1762). Clergyman in the Established Church, academic and Astronomer Royal from 1742. Nephew of Rev James Pound. Bradley carried out much of his astronomical research at Wanstead.

^{cxxxix} Lake House was built in the early eighteenth century as a banqueting house with guest accommodation for Wanstead House. It fell into a state of

sad neglect during the nineteenth century, and was demolished in 1908, after spending some years as home to a sports club. Its setting, the Great Lake, had been abandoned and largely drained by 1820 or so.

cxl Thomas Hood (1799-1845). Humorist and poet. Lived at Lake House, Wanstead, from 1832-1835.

cxli Grinling Gibbons (1648-1721). Dutch-born sculptor and wood carver widely regarded as the finest of his time. His work survives at Hampton Court, St Paul's Cathedral and in many smaller commissions. Horace Walpole wrote of him: "There is no instance of a man before Gibbons who gave wood the loose and airy lightness of flowers, and chained together the various productions of the elements with the free disorder natural to each species."

cxlii Jean-Antoine Watteau (1684-1721). A French painter known for his idyllic rustic scenes. Some of his other subjects were drawn from Italian comedy and ballet.

cxliii George III, King of Great Britain and Ireland (1738-1820: reigned 1760-1820). The union between Great Britain and Ireland took place in 1801. Early in George's reign, Great Britain defeated France in the Seven Years' War, and the treaties of Hubertusburg and Paris made it the dominant power in North America and India. However, many of the American colonies were subsequently lost in the American Revolution. A series of wars against revolutionary France, over a 20-year period, ended with the final defeat of Napoleon Bonaparte in 1815, though George was by this time too ill to be aware of the fact - a permanent regency had been in place since 1811.

cxliv Originally the setting for Upton House, West Ham Park was acquired in 1762 by philanthropist Dr John Fothergill, who established a botanical garden there. After Dr Fothergill's death, the Park passed into the hands of the Gurneys, a well-known Quaker family. They eventually sold it to the Corporation of London which opened it as a public park in 1874. Planters acquired at the sale of Wanstead House may still be seen in West Ham Park.

Why is Wanstead Park special?

Wanstead Park is the surviving remnant of one of England's most celebrated and influential gardens, upon which such eminent landscape designers as George London and Humphry Repton have left their mark. Important features of these gardens survive today, and Wanstead Park is a Grade II* listed landscape, meaning that it is regarded as being of national significance. The public park contains two individually listed buildings - the Temple and a ruined grotto (both Grade II). Wanstead Parish Church (Grade I) was also connected to the estate, and the stables of Wanstead House (Grade II) now house the Wanstead Golf Club.

Who are the Friends of Wanstead Parklands?

Reactivated in 2009, our mission is to raise awareness of the history of Wanstead Park, to conduct or commission original research into the park's history, and to campaign for its preservation and improvement.

More information on the Friends of Wanstead Parklands and their work may be found at http://www.wansteadpark.org.uk/
Join our mailing list for updates: info@wansteadpark.org.uk
Follow us on Facebook and Twitter (@FWP2009)